White Envelopes

by Marlee Garza

Printed in the United States of America

First Printing 2018

ISBN 978-1984357816

Create Space Publishing

Non-Fiction
Reader Beware -Due to the story content, may not be suitable for those 18 years of age and under. Parental guidance suggested. Contains sexually explicit subject matter.

www.justmarlee.com

Dedicated to

Brittnee, Michael, and Steffen:
Thanks for loving your mom through all the crazy years!

~~~~~~

All the "Conquerors" out there:
You are never alone!

~~~~~~

Contents

Foreword

Hi, Everyone! My name is Brittnee. I am Marlee's daughter.

The daughter of a creative, funny woman.
The daughter of a loyal friend.
The daughter of an amazing single mother.
The daughter of a former escort.

That last one always tends to raise an eyebrow. When I tell people, most of the time they lean in and eagerly start rattling off questions. This book will answer many of your questions. For now, here are some personal answers of mine to get you started:

Yes, she was open with me about escorting.

Yes, I was supportive of her choice.

No, I never considered joining the "family business."

I'm excited for you to read her story. I know the word, "prostitute" can have some negative connotations. For many, the topic of sex is difficult altogether. This story pushes boundaries and maps out what is, otherwise, a generally uncharted territory. The lighthearted tone of the writing will put readers at ease during what some might initially consider to be an uncomfortable topic. I hope it changes some stigmas that surround people who do certain things that are considered, "taboo."

Assuming it's because of the abuse she went through as a child, my mom was always adamant that she wanted my brothers and I to know our worth. To know we were loved. She encouraged us daily, never told us our dreams were too big, and helped us believe that we can achieve anything. Looking back nearly 30 years later, I'm extremely grateful for her guidance. Thanks to what she instilled in me, I've been able to successfully navigate the unpredictable world of the entertainment industry with optimism and self-assurance.

Our family went through some crazy, rough times. Those moments can either drive you apart or bring you together. In our case, it brought us together. We learned how to enjoy the good times and laugh through the bad ones. We called ourselves, "Team Garza" and let me tell you, Team Garza went on some serious adventures together. My mom made sure we remembered that when we couldn't rely on anyone else, we could always count on each other. She taught us core values like respect, kindness, faith, and perseverance. She taught us how to see things from other people's points of view. She taught us that, with every experience we have, there's a version of the story that will make us feel empowered.

Following my mom's example, I've picked up on the importance of finding healthy ways to define my relationship with the things that have happened to me in the past. Particularly with the more unsavory things. Unlike my mom, I wasn't sexually abused as a child, however, I've been a victim of poverty, bullying, homelessness, and other unpleasant circumstances that could have ruled my life. Instead, I chose to use those experiences as opportunities to provide the contrast which reminded me to appreciate my blessings. I chose not to be a "victim" of a "single-mother" lifestyle. I chose to love how perfect my family of four was: My mom, my two brothers, and me. Team Garza! I chose happiness, gratitude, and love. I slip and fall every now and then, but for the most part I have learned how to keep my head up. And I learned it from her.

In one way or another, we can all relate to being the victims of unfortunate circumstances. Maybe we've even done things in our past that we feel ashamed of. We become prisoners of our circumstances and mistakes. But it's time to break those chains.

Which is why I urge you to read on.

My mom is just a regular mom! Her past as an escort has no negative reflection on her character. The sex industry is often very different than the media portrays it, or how society views it. If there's one thing I'd want you to take away from this story, I would hope that it's inspiration. Inspiration to redefine the role that circumstances have played in your life. Inspiration to love others (and yourself!) unconditionally. Inspiration to take a step back and really take the time to see situations from other people's points of view. Most importantly, may this story remind you that you are valuable.

You are more than your circumstances.

Brittnee Garza, Actress/Artist

Introduction

I am not a famous person. My name isn't known throughout the world or even here in the United States. I'm not a household name in my local community. At this point I'm an unknown author. In fact, this book is my only finished one so far. I suppose I'd be viewed as just another average person alive on planet earth, trying to stay afloat in this uncertain world. I'm really no different than millions of others out there. I'm just "me"!

Everyone living on planet earth has a story. I definitely have a story and I share it in hopes of unveiling some truths based on my experiences, regarding a few misconceptions on some very touchy subjects in society, mostly about the world of escorting. This story is based on events that have taken place in my life.

I'm not a renowned expert on anything. I do not hold a degree in anything except perhaps the "school of hard knocks". I am not a Bible scholar, though I use some God references here and there and some Bible verses because Christianity is where I draw my foundational beliefs. God and my relationship with Jesus are important in my life. It is in those very foundations where I've been able to gain strength to get through the darkest and most painful times in my life.

I'm what our society calls "a survivor". I didn't survive the holocaust, or any other God-forsaken war story. I have never been held hostage or at gunpoint, knifepoint or anything like that. I've never been diagnosed with anything life-threatening or completely debilitating. However, I am a "survivor" of adversity, but I choose to say I am a *conqueror* of great adversity. That's how I choose to view myself; A conqueror; a warrior, a determined person who can get through anything. That's me.

I've always been like that. I suppose it was a defense mechanism somewhere in my psyche that triggered me to become such a fighter in my broken twisted world...

As a young girl, like millions of children out there have been, I was sexually abused on a regular basis by either relatives or a few neighbor boys. From my earliest memories until I was 10 years old sexual molestation was a regular occurrence in my life. Throughout my youth and into young adulthood my quest for acceptance and real love from a boy turned into an adolescence of promiscuity, stemming from the patterns set by the molestations of my early childhood.

In sharing this story, it's not really important to me to name the offenders who harmed me with their sexual deviancy. A few of them are dead anyway, and those still living know what they did and have had years of festering knowing that I know what they did to me. It is more important to share about how being conditioned as a child made it easy to fall into a promiscuous way of life that eventually led me decades later comfortably into the taboo world of prostitution as a high end escort in Seattle.

There was a time in my life for many years where I looked down on any form of prostitution. Someone close to me even was married to a former escort for a (very) short time. I was very vocal about what I thought of "girls like her"! Little did I know that about five years later after a few twists and turns in my life, I'd be in the same profession.

Lesson learned: Don't judge others until you have walked their path.

Sharing about my life as an escort is not a sad, "woe is me" tale to tell. For the most part I had wonderful experiences, learned a lot about myself and others, and can look back with little regret and lots of fondness. As with any job, it had positive and negative elements to it. I made a conscious decision to choose my "career" path. I knew what I was doing from the very beginning and was confident that I could and would be successful at it.

One of the strongest benefits of being an escort is that it gave me the freedom to be there for my kids at their crucial 'tween and teen ages, while giving us the means to have a better life than any $10 an hour job would. The only regret I have about it, is that I didn't have a better "business mind" and didn't save more money along the way. Instead I made sure that my three kids and I had a fabulous place to live in a community full of successful people and we lived well!

My kids grew up believing they deserved and could have everything they want if they put their mind to it and worked hard for it. They had great role models in their coaches, team parents, neighborhood families we knew, and by me being there for them and by them watching me run a successful business. We had one of the coolest places ever to live for a few years with fond memories and great stories to tell about it!

I met spectacular people during my years in the adult industry. I'll share some of the highlights and a few lower lights as well. Names are changed to protect identities. No need to expose people. That is not my intent. A lady such as I need never reveal names for personal gain. There is no point from my perspective to do so.

I wish to share my experiences with anyone who cares to read about them in hopes that they learn a little something. Perhaps my readers will see things from a different perspective, understand the world of escorting a bit differently, judge a little less harshly OR better yet, not judge anymore at all! Maybe some people will gain cool little tidbits that will help their marriage, relationships, and/or sex life. Hopefully something read here will give you a laugh, help you to be more comfortable with talking "sex" and maybe give you a confidence boost in the bedroom.

My perspectives are just that; Mine. My philosophy is, "*You* live your life the way you wish to and I'll do the same." Judgment is left in the hands of God. I choose to love all people; some people of course are easier to love than others. My approach to life is "No Guilt, No Shame, No Condemnation"! I do not dwell on my mistakes. There is no point. Forgiveness forgets; Plain and simple. **Live life with freedom.**

An amazing couple who are great pastor and happiness-coach friends of mine, taught me their philosophy of living life by using choices made through wisdom. If I had learned their precise way of operating in it when I was much younger, my life path might have been ridiculously different!

I'm happy to live by the wisdom philosophy now, yet I'm happy that I didn't before because being an escort was one of the best things that could have happened to me. It helped me gain control of an aspect in my life that was completely out of control for decades. It also taught me about my own character while giving me the ability to find the beauty in every person that I encountered. It showed me that everyone is different in their sexual wants and needs within a relationship, yet quite the same in their desires; namely to be loved, appreciated, accepted, and respected.

This book barely scratches the surface of my adventurous and unconventional life. Hopefully it will be enough to give a greater understanding into the world that has to stay hidden because it's unacceptable by society. I hope someday that it can come out of the dark because it has relevance and actually can help more than it hurts when handled in a proper manner. It's all in the approach. I approached it intelligently and gracefully. That's how and why I feel escorting worked to serve my life in a positive way for a few great years!

Whatever your sexual preference is makes no difference to me because I believe that is a personal decision. My belief is that God has created all of us and has given each of us freedom of choice based on the Wisdom we glean from His Word. That said, the information presented in this book is based mainly on heterosexual relationships; You may feel free to glean from it what you would like to for your own personal relationships.

**The following pages are filled with true accounts based on the events that have transpired throughout my entire life. Except for those used with permission, names have been changed because I'm not looking to expose or hurt anyone. Rather, I hope to help encourage people who read this to reach out in love to all people, to stop judging yourself and others, and to understand that through grace we truly can experience perfect and unconditional love and forgiveness. I also hope to give insight on an industry that has for decades been judged harshly and portrayed poorly in both the media and by Hollywood. I tell it from my perspective based on the things I experienced...

This is not to be deemed a "self-help" book, and anything I write here is simply my perspective on what I experienced in my life journey. I do not claim to be an expert. Any of my suggestions are just that; Suggestions based on what I've learned through my experiences along the way. We are all unique. Find what works for you. **

~~*~~*~~*~~*~~*~~*~~*~~*~~

...But Jesus bent down and started to write on the ground with His finger. When they kept on questioning Him, he straightened up and said to them, "If anyone of you is without sin, let him be the first to throw a stone at her...". At this, those who heard began to go away one at a time, the older ones first, until Jesus was left with the woman still standing there. Jesus asked her, "Woman, where are they? Has no one condemned you"? "No one sir", she said. "Then neither do I condemn you", Jesus declared, "Go now and leave your life of sin".

(John 8:6-11 New International Version)

~~*~~*~~*~~*~~*~~*~~*~~*~~

Off Into the Sunset

It was a poetic evening, preparing for my final escorting appointment as "Sandhal Banks", my alter-ego and one of Seattle's popular escorts for three and a half years. I was alone that night in our apartment in the quaint upper-crust community of Queen Anne Hill. My three teenage kids had their circles of friends to go hang out with so they left early that evening. As for me, I needed to get ready to go check into my hotel room; my incall at the time, for one last encounter. I packed my bags and dressed casually. Once I was completely ready, I donned my coat, grabbed my bags, and out the door I went.

I didn't have any money for the bus ride down to the hotel, so with my overnight bags and purse in hand, I walked from our apartment all the way down Taylor Avenue. It was a typical, rainy, early spring night in Seattle; dark, wet, chilly and a bit windy. I didn't have a car because the transmission on mine had gone out a few months before. Living in the city, the bus had become my mode of transportation. The rain was beating down on me and I was getting drenched. My rain-soaked long auburn hair was whipping fiercely around in the wind. To cars passing by me as I walked, I must have appeared to be a homeless lady shuffling to find her shelter for the night with her life's belongings in tow!

Sadly, I really wasn't far from being that described lady. After all, I was nearly broke and headed on foot down the hill to check into an inexpensive hotel so that at 10AM the following morning, for one last time, I would have a paid sexual encounter with my last stranger. But... Would I, after it was all said and done, have the strength to stop my life as an escort? I pondered this and several other thoughts about my three and a half years as an escort while I walked the half a mile down the hill to the hotel...

My last client arrived for his appointment with me promptly at 10:00 that next morning. He was a handsome man, taller than I was by a few inches, with brown hair and blue-green eyes. He was very friendly and fun to talk with. After talking with him for a while he shared that he was married. Several of my clients were married men, though many said they weren't. I asked him why was he seeing me then? I often asked my clients that question. Curiosity always got the best of me. The "detective" in me always liked to try and figure out the mystery of what was going on in homes around western Washington for all these husbands to seek out women like me to satisfy them sexually.

I told this gentleman that he was quite lucky to be seeing me. He asked why, so I told him that he was my very last client and that after our encounter was over that day, "Sandhal", my alter-ego extraordinaire, would be quietly fading away with not even a goodbye to the Seattle escorting community.

He asked how I had come to my decision and I boldly began to share about how God had woken me up from a dream state-of-mind nearly two weeks prior to him and I meeting. I shared with him that I was a Christian and how my life had spiraled out of control financially a few years prior. I told him how I couldn't find work anywhere and out of financial difficulty coupled with the seemingly bad luck I'd had throughout my life with dating men, that I researched the possibility of becoming an escort and boldly branded myself as a business! I shared with him about the great extent of researching the industry and then talking with a few people close to me about it and even having a conversation with God about my choice of doing that for a living until it was time to quit.

The look on his face while I was sharing my story with him was interesting. It was a mix of sheer intrigue and a hint of solemnness. I asked him if I had said something offensive (not that I really cared if I had), and he said "No". Then he proceeded to tell me that he was the worship leader of his church! Most people would have been shocked and perhaps disgusted that someone in ministry would go so far as to visit and pay an escort. Obviously, I wasn't going to judge him. I guess that when I was telling him why I was quitting he might have felt quite convicted upon hearing me share of how God had "woken me up." Maybe he felt as though he could open up to me since I had been so transparently honest with him. We were kindred...

We had an interesting chat for the rest of our time together. He opened up and shared some things about his life, marriage and work. We sat in silence for a time and when we made eye contact, we began to shake our heads and laugh about God's sense of humor. He (God) had orchestrated my very last client to be one who I had never met before, rather than one of my "regulars". That client, who I now refer to as "Choir Boy", was a fellow believer who was struggling in an area he was weak in and hopefully through that day he found strength for the future! It's as though God used that day to show both choir boy and me that he sees all and knows all, but the most important thing He wants us to understand, is that He *loves* all... No matter what!

I took the bus home after "Choir Boy" left my hotel room. I had money once again to do so. I left the room key on the table, gathered up my "Sandhal stuff" for the last time, glanced around the room while echoes of fond memories of amazing encounters began flashing through my mind, and simply walked down the hallway out the hotel door and waited for the bus to take me up the hill. Sandhal Banks was no more.

Off she rode (on a bus) into the sunset...

By the time I got home from the hotel I was very excited! I was heading in a new and different direction, and was excited to see what was in store for me. The next thing in line was to get a "normal" job again. I would wait a few weeks to allow myself a little break to transition from my secret world of escorting into being "just Marlee" once again...

Toddler to Twenties:
A Tumultuous Tale

When I was a young girl, I had aspirations of becoming a chiropractor and an orthodontist. I guess I had a strange fascination with the structure of the human body! Of course, like most little girls, I also dreamed of being in love one day with a perfectly handsome man; my own "Prince Charming".

To my recollection, never once did I dream that someday not only would I encounter hundreds of sexual partners in my life, but also fulfill my lifelong dream of becoming an escort or as some would call it, "A prostitute"!

As a young woman, if anyone had told me that escorting was going to be a future chapter in my life, I would have laughed them right out of the room. The chapter does exist and it's a very important part of my life now, just not in the "slap her on the wrist and don't do it again" or "Throw her in jail" way most people think it should be.

How I got to that chapter is rather complex...

~ Evaluating the events along the path of my life reveals a masterful patchwork quilt of emotion. It weaves trauma, laughter, tragedy, and joy with splashes of angst, triumph, pain, and hope, all of which encompass the hollow core of my heart where love should be encapsulated. Yet it's been a life lived by faith knowing that everything will be alright because I'm destined for greatness and deserving of love. ~

As a young girl, like millions of children out there, I was sexually or verbally abused on a regular basis by either relatives or a few neighbor boys. My parents, though they loved each other, had explosive tempers and fought with each other often enough to make an impact on my siblings and me. All of this happened during the time of my formative years.

When I was seven or eight years old we became a transformed happy church-going Christian family and things were pretty great at home for the next four or five years. When I was 11 years old my mom lost her six year battle with breast cancer and died in the summertime while I was away at church camp. Four months later my dad remarried per my mom's last wish which was, "Find a mother for my children".

Smoking pot and drinking to get drunk by age 12 was what I learned from my new step-siblings! It was something I hadn't been around much, but it was fun and exciting. At age 14, roller skating at our local roller rinks on a daily basis became my great escape activity. **There I could be whoever I wanted to be while I listened to the music and skated the days away.**

I "voluntarily" lost my virginity, that is I made the conscious decision to have sex with someone rather than them just molesting or raping me, as a 15 year old sophomore in an apple orchard. The 16 year old boy I gave it up to sadly was killed along with his best friend in a freak motorcycle accident about two months later. My dad divorced stepmom numbers one and two by the age of 17. I moved out on my own once I turned 18 and had a couple of crazy and irresponsibly fun years after that! By the time I was 20, I had racked up nearly 100 sexual partners in my life. Many of them, just for the fun of it, but lots of them in hopes that I'd actually get a boyfriend out of it!

Little Girl, Big Secrets

When I was just a little girl around four years old, it began. Years of sexual molestation, and rape; the grooming and conditioning that transpired from that tender young age until I was 10 would set the ball in motion for future years of allowing myself to be used by countless numbers of guys. I became the unofficial poster child of promiscuity!

Many of our relatives lived close by which made it convenient for lots of family get-togethers. The grown-ups would drink coffee, smoke cigarettes, and play cards in the kitchen. The older kids would all play outside or in the living room. One of the older male relatives would sit in his chair and watch TV. I'm not sure when it all started, but I can recall early memories of me being asked if I wanted to sit in his lap to watch television. I would just climb up onto his lap and we would watch whatever happened to be on the tv at the time. I remember he used to tickle or massage my legs. It was funny when he tickled me and it felt good when he massaged my legs.

Over time his hands began to wander around my body nonchalantly as I sat on his lap. Eventually he would touch places that even at my young age I knew were wrong, but in a strange way it felt good so I'd let him keep doing it. I guess this is where some "expert" would chime in and classify this as "conditioning". Looking back, I call it what it was; Sick and extremely twisted deviant behavior.

Eventually, it got to the point where he somehow figured out that he could get me to go to his bedroom with him and nobody would ever notice we were gone. There he would do all sorts of nasty things with me and tell me not to let anybody know if I wanted to be able to have the tingly feelings that felt so good. It would be our secret; I was his "special girl". Why that intrigued me then I still do not know! I suppose him causing me to have orgasms was the clincher. I had no clue what an orgasm was back then, but I had lots of them and he was the person who helped me have them. In some ways I hated him because deep down I knew he was a bad person, but the feeling I got from him touching me and doing things to me were addicting even at my very young age. These secret incestuous encounters went on for six years and probably only stopped because he died.

During that time, I had a few older cousins who seemed to somehow know that they could get me to allow them to do sexual things with me. They would bribe me with those old fashioned bubble gum cigars or shiny quarters in return for letting them put their hands down my pants or pull down my pants so they could touch and look at "me". Looking back as I write this, I'm thinking that was my introduction to my first "prostitution". I received money or a treat if I gave someone pleasure... Yes, sadly it was a sick and warped form of child prostitution.

There was another relative who once started to try something on me when I was younger.. Sometime during the middle of the night, while I was spending the night at their house after babysitting, I woke up to his hands and mouth on my developing breasts. I pretended to be asleep though my heart began to pound. I didn't know what to do. Had he realized I was awake? Did he know that I woke up aroused (I didn't even know that word at my age then!) even though I knew it was very wrong? Could he feel my heart beating faster? How could he be doing this too, just like all the others? "I must be a very nasty little girl and everyone knows it", I thought. I pretended to stir in my sleep and then turned toward the back of the couch. He must have gotten nervous so he went to bed. I laid there for a while thinking about how I was such a naughty young girl. Why? What was it that made everyone want to touch, fondle, or have sex with me? Why did I enjoy it when I knew it was wrong but they could make me tingle and feel so good? I was way beyond confused.

I was 10 years old.

Even the neighbor boys got in on the action! My dad had a landscaping business so there were always lots of trees around our yard. Easy to hide in, one of the neighbor boys pulled me in between a bunch of them one day. He then asked me if he could "feel" me and if I would like to "feel" him. I had already had this stuff done to me so many times and I knew I liked the feeling so I said "Yes". I'm pretty sure he was surprised that a young girl of my tender age of 11 knew how to "handle" him. We had several secret rendezvous around the neighborhood until he went away to college.

This all happened in an age where sexual abuse and incest were not talked about. Everything was kept as my dirty little secrets. I couldn't tell anyone about it. My sexuality had developed before my body had! I was masturbating every day, every chance I could. Most little girls while in their room played with their Barbies or other dolls and toys. I played with my body! I would fantasize about some cute boy and then the touching of myself would begin.

My main abuser used to insert different objects inside of me to make me orgasm and showed me how I could do the same to myself. Looking back, now I get that he was just a huge pervert who probably got off watching a child masturbate! Literally, as I was typing this I figured that out. On one hand so sexual, on the other, I'm still naive!

There were some cute older high school-aged boys that moved next door to us. It was the 70's and they were "long haired hippies" as my dad called them. Well, I decided I liked "long haired hippies"! I was extremely attracted to them.. I always wished they would invite me over and fantasized that they did. I might have been a young pre-teen, but by then I was addicted to sex; Mostly either masturbating or oral sex; most of the time receiving, occasionally giving. I wanted it to happen all of the time, and I had no idea how to stop myself and my feelings!

I was 12 years old.

After my mom died, my dad married a really nice lady who had four kids of her own which made us an instant "Brady Bunch" type of family. I had a stepbrother who had a very cute friend named Jerry that he would invite to stay over on Friday nights. Jerry and I had a mutual crush on each other when we first met. I was 12 and he was a "more experienced" 15 year old. He was cute and funny and was really cool to have around! He taught me how to French kiss. I hadn't ever been kissed on the mouth by a boy I actually liked until the first time Jerry kissed me. Though it was kind of slobbery, it was fun to kiss a boy that was near my age and one I was genuinely attracted to.

During that first encounter with him, we "made out" while the song "Hooked on A Feeling" played. My record player was set to continue to play the record over and over.. It did so for about an hour. Jerry never did try to touch my body; he just tenderly kissed me with his arms gently wrapped around me. That song playing while we kissed impacted me that day so much that music became a very important element in my life for getting past anything negative that I needed to overcome.

Jerry lived too far away and was nearing high school while I was just about to enter the 7th grade, so we never had another moment like that. But I thank God for him because Jerry was the one boy who helped me realize that all the people who had touched me before him were horrible and had no business doing that to me. I realized that I had been allowing people to get away with things that they never should have been doing. I'm not completely sure how I came to that epiphany, but Jerry's kiss, you might say, woke me up!

Unfortunately I still had nobody to talk to about everything I had been through. I kept going on through life thinking I was fine. After all, by this point I had my foundational belief in God, I had made it through the death of my mom, I was "grown up" and was now cooking dinner for the family and responsible for many chores. I was a survivor of what I had begun learning was a terribly heinous thing called sexual abuse (but still nobody knew about my hidden secrets). I was strong and I had survived.

I was 13 years old.

I spent the majority of my life allowing guys to have full use of my body in a sexual manner. As a little girl, when I was being molested it was difficult to rationalize the right and wrong of what my relatives and neighbor boys were doing to me. I only knew that the end result sent my body into this thing that made me feel really good and I liked that feeling. I was having orgasms before I even learned my ABC's & 123's! That is crazy, I know, yet it is truth about my childhood. How does a child grow up to be "normal" after that?

They don't.

Eventually I figured out that what was happening to me was not only wrong, it was something that was presented as "shameful". Only bad or naughty girls did those kinds of things. "Sluts" did those things. Being known as a slut wasn't something admirable. Back then I was told by my offenders (and we've all heard this before!) that it was my fault that these things happened. They all said that they couldn't help themselves from wanting to touch me because my body was so desirable.

WHAT? I was a little girl; a child with no boobs, curves, or anything remotely sexy or sensual going on! But blame, shame, and guilt reared their ugly heads. I had "dirty little secrets" that I couldn't tell anybody about without the fear of getting in trouble or being shamed by the people in my life.

Those heinous actions of child molestation against me set the course for a life of promiscuity... It was always the same; Meet a guy, like a guy, guy gets horny because I was "so sexy they couldn't help it"... Little voice inside my head, like a stuck record player, would say, "Marlee, you're a naughty girl. It's your fault they're horny so you'd better make them happy (satisfy them)."

In the depths of my heart that girl with the buried secrets always hoped that if I was really nice, funny, creative, talented, and pretty, combined with being super good at sex, that the boys I liked would see that I was worth keeping and even more, worth loving! It's been my lifelong quest; Hope that a boy (now, at my age, a man) might someday love me for just "me" instead of wanting me for their sexual gratification. The difference now is that I get to be super picky.

Jesus Loves A Slut Like Me

Interestingly, throughout my years of promiscuity, I always had an innocent childlike optimism and the gift of laughter (I still do)! Even though I had been jokingly dubbed a slut by my friends and I eventually embraced the title and rocked it, I also had this view that Jesus loves me even with my extreme slut status. He would always be there. Maybe it was the type of spirit born within me. For decades now I've said, "Daddy God will handle everything because He loves and forgives me no matter what". It's the way I've always believed.

Childlike faith!

Laughter has always been the source for my strength. Joy in simply knowing that God loves me "just as I am" built great strength within me from my earliest days of learning who He is. That is the conquering power I've used to get through tough times.

Jesus took care of the "garbage" of our lives at the cross! Boom! Done! I always felt like it was selfish of me to hold onto unforgiveness or those three inhibitors; guilt, shame and condemnation. Otherwise the point of Jesus getting the crap beat out of him, then publicly ridiculed and shamed, pounded with spikes and hoisted up to bleed to death on the cross is rendered pointless! Since I believe Him to have lived that destiny, then I need to just let it go; Whatever "it" is. So I willingly have accepted his forgiveness and tried my best to not allow past mistakes to haunt or taunt me. Instead I try to live my life doing the things that bring me happiness and lots of laughter, trusting the voice of Wisdom to be my guide.

Choose To Be A Conqueror

Somehow, that still small voice inside of me gave me the endurance for what I was going through. Feelings of heartache, being unlovable, despicable, unwanted, tainted, and unworthy would surface at times but not stay for very long. I never really felt hatred or anger toward the male relatives who took away my innocence or invaded my privacy. Once I realized that they were sick, warped, and twisted, I viewed them as icky and had no reason to want them in my life. I still view them as such, but in my heart many years ago I forgave them. I did that for me, so I wouldn't become bitter and prevent myself from having joy, peace, and happiness.

Not only did I survive all the years of the heinous acts against me, but I made it my personal goal to conquer the *demons* who lurked in the darkest corners of my mind. The reason I like calling myself "conqueror" rather than a survivor is because I don't want to just survive. That's like just hanging on. Hanging on is good, but giving the extra push, a war cry, the thing that says, "I will beat this down and squelch it from the existence in my life!" is more of a conqueror's spirit; That's what I have done and how I continue to live!

I want people to understand, as I have learned over the years, that they can choose to climb to the top, and even if they slide down a bit or all the way down, keep climbing without giving up, make it to the mountain top and proudly stand firm in who they are... and while they're at it take a look at the view because it's much more ominous and beautiful from the top than down at the bottom!

Even in my darkest moments of abuse, I somehow knew I wasn't going to let the users and abusers beat me down. I have a true warrior's spirit in me! If you let yourself be "victimized", that is, allowing the situation to take over and rule the course of the rest of your life journey, it then becomes your fault if you don't get out of that mindset. I know heartache, all types of abuse, the bad things that happen in our lives can hurt tremendously. Believe me, I understand pain from such things. It takes time to heal, but it is so much easier if you can just truly let it go. The best way for that is through forgiveness... Forgiveness of others as well as yourself, which can be tough.

Often the victimizer goes on about their life after they've left you with the wounds or scars... They don't even think twice about what they did to you. Therefore, we must try to release them and their inflictions so they don't penetrate into our souls, polluting our spirit.

The pain-free scars remain in me and serve as a reminder of my courage and strength. It's like a favorite Bible verse of mine (*Genesis 50:20* ~ *"You intended to harm me, but God intended it for good to accomplish what is now being done; the saving of many lives").* My scars have been transformed into beauty marks by God. They are embedded into the very essence of who I am; A mighty warrior princess who has battled fiercely in many wars, not without wounds, left with scars, healed, strengthened, and refreshed; armed and ready for battle to help save others from the fall!

Crazy circumstances beyond my control as a child are what has led my life since then down a winding path with many crossroads to choose from. Sometimes I chose the right and peaceful path leading to joy and contentment. Other times I ended up in a savage-filled wilderness or trekking blindly around a grand lonely mountain trying to find my way back to a safe familiar road! My journey has always been one full of adventure. The biggest and most rewarding was the one that follows...

A Decision Made

On a December day in 2002, just a few days before Christmas, I was called into my boss' office at the divisional headquarters of The Salvation Army where I worked as an administrative assistant. Unfortunately they had the undaunted task of giving me the word that I'd be laid off at the end of the year. The financial fallout from 9/11 had taken its toll a year later on charitable contributions across the nation and The Salvation Army was not immune to that hardship. At the time, I wasn't worried about it because God had always been faithful and provided me with what was needed; in this case a new job.

When the New Year rolled around I was laid off as planned. I actually applied for unemployment but was turned down because of one minor detail: The Salvation Army is a non-profit organization therefore they do not pay into that system and I was understandably rendered ineligible to receive unemployment benefits.

So began my quest for a new job. The "job hunt" was always an easy thing for me. Workplaces usually found me, rather than me going in search of them. Whether it was word of mouth from a friend or my sparkling personality gaining attention from a manager from some other business while they were patrons where I happened to be working at the time, I never lacked in having a potential new job. That is until 2003 rolled around!

I began my job search in mid-February of that year, after the rejection came in from the unemployment office. I applied at a few shops on Queen Anne Hill, an affluent neighborhood, where my kids and I were living at the time. Then I applied at a few car dealerships, several offices, some clothing stores, a few larger retailers, restaurants, delivery services, wine distributors, and various other establishments. There were 56 places I applied to from February through June and there were 56 rejections that coincided with those applications. One of them included a potential guest service job with the most known icon of Seattle's skyline and their tourism attractions. I had a great job history with excellence in customer service. I also had on my resume some years with one of the greatest entertainment companies in the world, yet I could not seem to land a job in tourism or any other line of work.

By July, my finances were shot; my bank accounts were depleted. I had gone on family assistance for food stamps and medical benefits. I refused to receive monthly cash assistance from the state as I felt that once I completely locked in to the welfare system I would somehow fall into the "dependence mentality" that seems to go with becoming a recipient of that type of help. I was determined to make it on my own with my three kids, while keeping us in a great neighborhood.

Sometime in early August, I was visiting my friends at the local fire station where they worked. They were aware that I had been out of work for several months and my friend Brad asked me how the job search was going. I answered him and the rest of the crew on duty telling of my recent job search rejections. He jokingly told me I should look in the ads at the back of a local Weekly publication that was sitting on the table; The ads geared for adult entertainment purposes! They all agreed I was sexy enough to be enticing for such jobs as were listed in the paper. Of course they were only kidding around about me doing anything like that. I laughed and said, "Yeah, I'll get right on that!", then proceeded to pick up the paper and read some of the things listed. There was an ad that caught my eye, but I didn't let on to the guys that I actually would even consider those listings as potential for an occupation.

On the way home that evening, I pulled up outside of our local corner market near our house and grabbed the two free weekly papers they had there. When I got home, I pulled up the website listed on that ad I was interested in. It seemed legitimate enough so I emailed my interest to the address provided. I got an answer the next day of what the job involved. It was an all-day photo shoot for an adult pay website where I would bring 10 outfits. With each "look" I would start fully clothed and bit by bit the articles of clothing would come off creating a series of fully clothed to fully naked pictorials for members of the website to view.

I've always been comfortable in my skin enough to prance around naked so I was not at all intimidated with doing the project. The pay for the job clinched the deal for me. For a fun day frolicking around I would make $500 cash. I did the job, had a blast and got paid. It was so natural and easy for me to pose nude. It was in many ways a huge turn on knowing that in the middle of the daylight hours I was there at this suburban house on some neighborhood street in Seattle, immersed in such naughty behavior. It was a rush!

I had always wanted to be in Playboy as a young girl because the centerfolds were always so beautiful and perfect. Although this wasn't exactly Playboy, it was something that allowed me to be in my element where I truly was incredibly comfortable. Unfortunately it was only a one-time deal. That's when I began my quest for my next option in adult entertainment, which of course is how I then got into my chosen career as an escort.

I'm a firm believer that all things happen for a reason. Whether good or bad there are always things to glean from each experience in life. Deciding to go down the pathway leading me into the world of escorting was a bold decision for me to make. It was a well thought out plan that evolved from a series of events that had left me with that all too familiar feeling of not being good enough to be loved; only good enough for sex...

I had experienced an interesting year where I decided it was time for me to begin dating again since my kids were at the age where I felt they were able to understand me wanting to do so. Online dating was all the rage so I joined a few of those dating websites and opened up my heart to the possibilities of finding "Mr. Right". I didn't really have the best of luck in finding him or anyone else decent in my online dating quest, but I tried several times anyway for about a year and a half.

Around that same time I also had met and was incredibly fond of someone who worked in emergency services in our community. He was a person who quickly became very special to me but very toxic to me as well. There was a chemistry we had that needed no words. It was pure raw power between us. I ended up falling head over heels in love with the man my friend Brynn dubbed "Cookie Man" because we didn't know his name when we first knew of him, but we knew he liked cookies! Cookie Man and I had a silent "thing". Intense attraction was there but nothing ever could happen between us. Bad timing sucks! I always thought someday together we would be a force to be reckoned with. Instead, his ability to pulverize my heart over the course of a couple of years, was a force that helped drive me with powerful velocity right into escorting!

Simultaneously when I first started to seriously contemplate becoming an escort, I was weaning myself from online dating. All my attempting to date had really done for me was led to several meet-ups with what I would eventually figure out to be married men. They never admitted it to me, but it's not rocket science to figure out the "married man thing"! There were also the usual jerks looking for one-night stands and even one guy who clearly was not the guy in the pictures on his profile! I met businessmen with profiles who were pretending to be single and hoping for free sex, and the topper; the guy who promised me a car if I would have sex with him and fly back east to be his trophy girl for some convention... I did have sex with him after getting really drunk, but I did not fly anywhere with him and I didn't get the car... most likely because he got the sex first which of course was his intent all along!

That guy however was pivotal in helping me to decide that if I was going to only find jerks to date then I might as well look into escorting. Also since my firefighter friends had suggested to me to contemplate the possibility of adult entertainment, and Cookie Man had shredded my heart, it was a perfect segue of timing for me to take the escorting ball and roll with it; to finally get paid to play!

At the time it was my wicked sense of humor talking, but at the same time I was running very low on money and needed to do something quickly. I was getting very annoyed and frustrated with men, myself, and my mundane poverty stricken life. By this contemplative time, I had already done the one-time website photo shoot and the $500 I earned for that wasn't enough to live on for very long.

So it was, that I began my quest to do what I was really good at and instead of giving it away for free, I was now going to make money; lots and lots of money, by having sex with men!

Research and Development Of My Alter-Ego Lifestyle

Why each person enters into the world of prostitution, is a very individual decision. I do believe that each one of us goes into it hoping to make money, and have fun, then once finished, come out healthy, alive, and able to move on to our next chapter of life. I can't speak for anyone who is or has been a sex worker or a sex "provider" except for myself. I can only tell about my experience and *choice* that I made to become an escort.

I'm aware that some people have been lured or tricked into being a prostitute. Usually hookers or streetwalkers are forced into it by someone who has made a false promise to them. Sometimes they end up having to "work" to pay off a drug debt, or maybe a client in a strip club has actually been a pimp disguised as a potential suitor genuinely interested in them, only to find out they have become indebted to a predator. Or sadly, the worst case that has become a worldwide disgusting epidemic is they may be a victim of human trafficking.

Let me say strongly and boldly: It is my opinion that ALL who participate in having sex with anyone against their will or with those who have no say so (Traffickers, clients of traffickers, rapists, sexual deviants, etc) deserve the worst kind of punishment that law of the land will hand down (plus castration)!

When I became an escort, it was not because I was tricked by any person. For me it wasn't an overnight decision. I talked it over with my close friend, Helga, my daughter Brittnee (who was only 13 at the time), and my brother. I had considered becoming a stripper, but after extensively speaking with my brother who had previously been a bouncer at a popular local strip club chain, I opted to go with escorting because it was a safer option. He had told me that some strippers end up being stalked and it becomes dangerous for them. Men can't touch these girls who dance; at least not in the Seattle clubs where they have a four foot law in place. On occasion there are men who get frustrated because they can't touch their fantasy girls and sadly some of them become so obsessed with the dancers that they will wait for them to be off shift and in their cars. Then the stalker guys follow the dancer home. My brother didn't want that to happen to me. I certainly didn't want to endanger Brittnee or my two boys, Michael and Steffen who at the time were 10 and 11. Escorting seemed the best and safest option for me to try.

Research for becoming a sex provider started soon after that conversation. Helga, Brittnee, and I read articles on the internet and studied many of the local escorts and escort services. We must have looked at a couple dozen websites to see what escorts looked like, the hours and days they worked, how much money they made for an hour or more of their time and companionship, and we looked at their ages to see if I was too old. My biggest fear was that at age 41, nobody would want to spend time with me.

Since I didn't know exactly how to get started on my own in the beginning, I emailed a service and asked if they thought I was too old or if they would be interested in the possibility of me becoming one of their girls. I was asked to send some recent photos, so I sent some of the pictures that I was allowed to keep from my naughty website photo shoot that I had just done.

I included one photo where I was lying on a couch with a beautiful deep blue velvet gown on. One of my legs was resting up on the back of the couch so you could see my bare lower region. The reply to my email and photos was, "You are stunning and you have the most beautiful lady-parts I've ever seen! My clients will enjoy meeting you"! I was both flattered and somewhat embarrassed, however, I emailed her back right away because I was eager to get the ball rolling, so to speak! We made a downtown lunch date for a couple days later to make sure everything was safe, good, and a pleasant professional working relationship would be had.

I was so broke at that point in my life that I had to borrow money from Helga for parking the day I went to lunch. I met Caryssa that day and she would be my boss for the next eight months. We had a delicious and very fancy lunch. Then we walked around a well-known tourist place in the city and shared some laughs and flirty fun with the street vendors along the way, including Caryssa grabbing my booty in front of them. Until that day I had never had a girl grab my tush; and in public at that!

While we were out and about that afternoon, Caryssa asked me if I wanted to try going out on an appointment that night. Of course I said I would, so she came up with an alter-ego name for me and so began life for "Kendra"! I ended up meeting with two different gentlemen that evening. At the end of the night I came home with $400 cash. I went out the next night and brought home $525. I believe I made that amount on the third night as well and by then I was hooked! Within three evenings I had gone from being flat broke to making $1450.00! My kids and I danced around with gleeful shrieks holding so much cash in our hands. Of course at the time Brittnee knew what I was doing, but my boys who I felt were too young to completely grasp the concept didn't really know what I did but they didn't care either. All they knew was we finally had money again!

Once I began building clientele, I quickly learned that my age was incredibly desirable. "MILFs" were really popular at the time with younger guys and many of the middle-aged and older men were interested in me because we had so much more "life stuff" in common. They could relate to me more easily than they could with a 20-something aged girl. The fact that I was articulate and well-mannered along with being attractive helped me to become popular. Well that along with my mad sexual skills!

Money, Power, & Confidence

After a few months of learning the ropes on being a great and popular provider, I realized that secretly for me this was what had become retribution time for all of the pain and damage from the sexual abuse of my childhood; the very reason I felt for most of my life I was put on the planet; to be a sex object for all men. I could now be their sex object, but now it was my turn to get something out of it for me... From now on, for men to be able to touch me, they had to pay me a lot of money! Hundreds of dollars an hour was my rate and often times these men booked several hours, just so they could be with me! It was my own sweet revenge against the sexual abusers of my childhood, the many men and even the boys from my past out there; All who had used and discarded me over the years for whatever reason. I was finally in the control seat. I had the power to say "yes you get to touch me; for a price". Or I had the power to say, "no, you don't get to spend time with me or have sex with me!". **My decision, my choice, my way!**

After 35 years of sexual misfortune, I had finally become the CFO of my vagina!

It wasn't that I hated men, I just hit a point in my life where it was past time for me to take control of my body. Getting paid to do the thing that so many had taken for granted for decades supercharged my psyche. I felt empowerment for the first time. I looked great, I felt amazing, and I strutted around town with an air of confidence that caused men's pants to bulge and women's nostrils to flare. I had "it" goin' on and I didn't have a care!

I was grateful toward almost every client I encountered. I had some wonderful men I spent time with who I just naturally enjoyed hanging out with. The ladies, other escorts, that I became friends with were phenomenal as well! They were kind, easy going, and so darn much fun! There are men and women currently who I am still friends with who used to be clients or provider friends of mine. The (former) clients of mine no longer exchange money for sex with me. Their lives have changed in various ways just as mine has. The children are all grown up and maybe they're now married with their own kids, their marriages may have ended and they've since married others, or like me, moved away to a different state, or changed jobs. Typical life-stuff because they're regular people just living life! I don't really see them, but they are friends that I still talk to or text, and maybe even have them as friends on social networking sites so we can always remain in touch because real lasting friendships were made!

A Name for Myself:
Sandhal Takes On Seattle

As with any job there are pros and cons in being an adult provider. Overall my life improved tremendously in the course of the years spent in that industry.

When I first started escorting we lived in the house of a 93 year old gentleman I used to home-care for. He ended up in a nursing facility but my kids and I were allowed to remain in his home until a few months after his death. During that time I was able to save up some money, to purchase furniture, clothing, food, and also pay my bills effortlessly.

When we were forced to move from that house for about two months, during the summertime we lived with our friend Lisa; A super cool single mom who had three daughters. They also lived on Queen Anne Hill. Brittnee and Lisa's oldest daughter Jaz were school friends which is how we first met. She kindly opened up her home to us.

Lisa knew what I did for a living and found it to be fascinating rather than repulsive. It was nice to know I had someone outside of the industry in my corner. During the short time we lived at Lisa's it was easy for me to focus on my new business. I had parted company with Caryssa's agency on friendly terms and was embarking on my own solo adventure as an escort. I needed to create a website to begin building a whole new clientele of my own in a completely different way. I was able to set my computer up there and the 14 year old girls Brittnee and Jaz, and I began to design and build my first website. We ran into a few roadblocks so I found a wonderful young and handsome client friend of mine who understood html code and writers, so he came over and finished the site for me. Once it was complete, my new and favorite alter-ego "Sandhal Banks" was born!

Caryssa kindly spent several hours by phone coaching me on how to be successful and safe as a solo call girl. Then came the amateur yet effective Sandhal photoshoot for my website. After that the advertising for my business started. For discretionary purposes I won't say where and how I advertised and built up my client base but there are safe venues to do so. Once people caught on that "Kendra" was now "Sandhal", business began to soar. My time and companionship was becoming very popular and in demand.

While living at Lisa's house, a mystery person contacted CPS and told them that Lisa was running a brothel in her home. It was absolutely ridiculous to me that someone would go to such lengths to potentially ruin people's lives. I'm pretty sure I know who it was though it was never confirmed. Because of that situation, I was forced to move out immediately so Lisa wouldn't have any further hassles.

I began living in a comfortable hotel in Seattle. It was also used as my "office" for most appointments with my clients. The kids loved it because it was a relaxed atmosphere there at the hotel and they had a pretty amazing breakfast buffet set up every day! The kids moved there with me around the time school started. They had the luxury of eating a big healthy breakfast and then I'd then drive them to school. After dropping them off, I was free to welcome appointments during the day until school was out. The kids would use one of the lobby areas to do homework after school on the rare occasion of my appointments overlapping with school being out. Once my workday was done we would do whatever activities were on our calendar; football practice, play rehearsals, or anything else we had to do. We led a fairly normal life in the hotel except we had daily maid service!

One of the best parts of having my own business and making good money at it was being able to be there for my kids for their athletics and school functions. Prior to my becoming an escort, there was a point where I had to work at four part time jobs to barely squeak by in life.

Suddenly I was able to work an hour or two a day and have the rest of the time to spend investing into my children's lives. It was a win-win situation for us.

It was about two months of living in that hotel when we ended up being approved to move into the penthouse of a brand new high end apartment complex overlooking Lake Union in Seattle. Having lived at hotels for a few months I was unable to save a lot of money toward the first, last, and deposit for an apartment. I was very "low volume" in my daily escorting appointments; most days only seeing one gent because I preferred my vagina to not have various visitors in a day if at all possible!

To get into the place that we had found and were excited to move into, an amazingly talented and generous client friend of mine helped pay for the deposit. Our rent was $3,100 a month, but I was able to maintain our lifestyle there for a couple of years. I had built quite a lucrative business with a strong repeat client base.

Sandhal's Lair

At last, I had my own incall. Our new place became both our home as well as my business. It was perfect because it was a top floor penthouse apartment with a stellar view overlooking Lake Union and a view of the north side of downtown Seattle including The Space Needle. There were two levels. so upstairs was "home" and downstairs was where my "Sandhal Lair" could be found. I loved my little cave of wonders where magical things happened, including the little white envelopes full of 20's, 50's and 100's that would magically appear on my bedside table!

~~*~~*~~*~~*~~*~~

The white envelopes are how an escort is paid. It's a known thing for those who participate in the "Hobby" of escorting. The clients are paying for "time and companionship" since paying to have sex with someone is illegal. The client will leave the envelope in a visible place, (usually the nightstand) so the lady will know she has received payment. It is never discussed beyond that. Most women double check the envelope when the gentleman excuses himself to use the restroom to assure her that she has been paid. Of course with repeat clients she knows she can trust, it isn't an issue and she purely enjoys the company while he is there!

~~*~~*~~*~~*~~*~~

My room; the master bedroom, was painted in deep plum. I had shimmery burgundy bedding, crushed velvet throw pillows, and gorgeous deep maroon curtains with beaded accents. There were deep red and purple accessories, iron candle holders, burgundy lighting and framed erotic flower prints on the walls. It was a sexy temptress' lair where all sorts of interesting encounters would take place for the next couple of years.

The bedroom had an adjacent bathroom with a nice oversized shower area and one of those contemporary "rain shower" shower heads. For my clients, I always had great amenities on hand readily available for them on the vanity (even if my incall was at a hotel I had my own supplies) so they felt at home and comfortable. Of course I always had a stack of fresh clean towels and washcloths. For their convenience I would supply disposable combs, toothbrushes, toothpaste, razors, mouthwash and small disposable cups, scented and unscented body wash, shampoo & conditioners. For most gents, I also would supply an array of beverages like juices, flavored waters and bottled water and even light snacks (for energy purposes, of course)!

It was always important to me to share a gift of hospitality to the men I encountered. It's how I am in both my personal and professional worlds; It's just a very big part of who I am.

As Sandhal, I was very well known for being kind, friendly, welcoming, engaging, and hospitable. Not bad for someone who at the time the rest of the world, had they known my occupation, might have viewed as just some insignificant   low-life   prostitute!

Perks of the Job

Besides being able to afford cool things and live in really nice places, there were personal benefits for me while being a provider. I was ages 41-44 when I did this work, but I looked like I was in my early 30's. I had plenty of time to work out. I was able to afford great quality food. The low carb lifestyle was very "in" at the time so that is how I ate. I felt wonderful. I constantly received compliments of what great hair I had. I had very little stress in my life at last, so I looked refreshed all the time.

The biggest perk and best thrill for me was knowing I was getting paid to have orgasms! Best job ever! Knowing that meeting a man would give me a white envelope with cash in it and that I was going to have my socks rocked off was enough to make me "ready" for all of my appointments. Many times while lying on the bed making small talk, my mind would drift to the concept of making great money for doing the activity I enjoy most! It never got old for me to think, "I'm getting paid for mutual sexual satisfaction!

I'll say it again; BEST job ever!

The thrill of my secret life made it that much more enticing to me to keep doing it. On one hand it was tough because I did not want my kids to go through embarrassment of the wrong people finding out and them losing friends. Through another incident in our lives about four and a half years before I became an escort, we ended up losing most of our friends at no fault of our own, because we were victims of voyeurism at the place we called home and had to abruptly move away. I didn't want a similar experience to happen with my being an escort.

I was known as one of few hot single moms on Queen Anne. Very few people knew what my occupation was. I had a theory that many of the dads whose kids played sports with mine recognized my face but could never really ask me if I was Sandhal. So it was just my tawdry little secret and it was a rush. Most of the moms were too uptight to even have a clue about me. I was alright with that too. I was having lots of fun just being "me" prancing around in my carefree way while so many of them were going through the motions of life and marriage, yet I was aware enough to see right through their misery. Sometimes I wished I could tell them what I did for a living so I could offer advice about intimacy and perhaps help them get their *sexy* back, but I knew they couldn't handle knowing that I was a sex worker.

Eventually, as time passed, the more I told my friends about my "job", against my wishes, they told other people and then those same friends began distancing themselves from me. It was sad and frustrating to realize the fragility of the information about my occupation. People can't handle the truth! I lost one of my best friends over my career choice and it was one of the friends who originally helped me meticulously enter the adult industry. I had friends of friends tell them they need to disassociate themselves from me. I found it so odd that people could be so easily influenced by others judgmental opinions instead of standing their ground based on how they actually felt. They were so easily swayed by someone who instantly judged based on their perspectives rather than on true and factual information about an occupation that they knew nothing about; except for what they'd seen on television or in movies!

The flip side to that is I also had incredibly supportive friends along the way who I never doubted had my back. One group of friends in particular were three friends from my old church. On a particular occasion, my friend Pam, who had moved to Texas a few years prior to my crazy lifestyle beginning, gathered two of our other friends on a visit to Seattle and the three of them met up with me at a lovely Italian restaurant at the top of Queen Anne. We were seated and ordered our food.

While we waited for dinner to arrive we played catch up with each other's lives. One by one each shared everything going on in life with work, family, their husbands, the kids, church, and whatever else seemed important to share about. The three of them were married with kids. I was single with kids. The three of them shared first, and then came my turn. When the question was asked of where I was working, I looked at all three of them and I said, "Well I am actually working as an escort". The looks on their faces were of sadness at first. I remember seeing tears well up in their eyes. Then I said to them, "Please don't be sad. It was my choice to do it, I make a great living and I'm pretty successful at it." My attitude toward escorting immediately put them at ease. Rather than it being a terrible thing for my life, I understood how nicely it was serving my kids and me. That's what Pam and the other two sensed as well. I never felt a negative or judgmental vibe from them. They didn't scoff or condemn me. After the initial shock of my surprising and unexpected story, then came the number one question that even now I always get asked; "So what is it like?" And from there the dialogue would begin. I would always and still do answer every question as honestly and thoroughly as possible.

It's always nice to know you have a friend who will pray for you no matter what! Ever since my kids were toddlers my friend Roxie has been an amazing spiritual and emotional support for me. She and I had both been there for each other through some very difficult seasons of each other's lives. We both made it past our situations and came out stronger having weathered the storms. She was a person I knew I could trust wholeheartedly.

There weren't very many people in my life I felt I could trust with the information of my having become an escort. People really wanted to be understanding and at first they usually were "cool with it" until they had time to fully digest the information I had given them! That is when they suddenly would become too busy to hang out with me or they would get all awkward if I was around. It was sad because I was still the same person who for a time simply had an unconventional occupation.

Roxie was always and still is the kind of friend who loves to pray for people. I decided it might be good to have a friend I could count on to pray for me but that also meant I needed to be straight with her and tell her what I was doing for a living.

I went to her house one evening and we left to go have a chat. She and I loved girl chats; Always having fun laughing at ourselves and our ridiculous antics. This time was different because I had to tell her about escorting. I had two ways of telling people what I did for a living, if I was sharing about my escorting with them. I would either blurt it out matter-of-factly or lead into to it slowly.

With Roxie, I tried to gently tell her because she has such a sweet spirit and cares so deeply for loved ones so I knew it would make her sad once she found out. I was right. As I was telling her about it her eyes welled up with tears that began quickly rushing down her cheeks. Of course I told her not to cry but then cried too! I felt bad that I had made her feel so sad. I reassured her that I was fine and I would come out of it alright. She hugged me and in her sweet loving voice said she was going to up her prayers for me and the kids and then simply said, "I love you". Never once did she get weird and she has always been consistently the same amazing friend!

It's All In How
You View It

From my perspective, escorting which is my strict focus since it is what I personally was involved in, is an industry that has been, for hundreds of years, sorely misunderstood!

Sure, there are seedy and shady elements to it because prostitution itself is illegal and therefore unprotected by the law. Of course, bad apples are found in every bunch. There are jerks out there; Both men and women who like to rip people off or cause harm or injury to another person and do so without hesitation or remorse. Those people are far and few between and can show up anywhere; not just in the sex industry. Sadly there are the misguided people who need to take drugs or get drunk to be involved in this career choice and then become super messed up! The rotten apples are few in the full spectrum of that side of the industry, at least in my experience.

Our society as a whole looks down it's judgmental nose at the people who participate in the exchange of money for sex. We've been taught to believe that the business of prostitution, including escorting, is for low-life people. Of course, in movies and television they mainly portray the standard "hookers on the streets" scenarios. I'm certain that several times when I've told friends or family members that I was an escort, that they first pictured me on some street corner near an alley wearing some tight mini dress with a feather boa and clunky platform shoes, and a curly bleached blonde wig! That's what we see in the movies or television shows, so it makes sense. If it's a show with a high priced call girl, then she either ends up dead, or a pawn in some twisted rich guy's game, or a hooker gone high end call girl like in "Pretty Woman" (I love that movie, but unfortunately it doesn't happen quite like that in real life).

When high profile busts of Hollywood celebrities, professional athletes and politicians occur, the "Johns" are always made out to be scumbags. The news media has a heyday with the sensationalizing of those stories, when in reality it's really an invasion of privacy! What consenting adults do on their own time is their business and nobody else's!

I've always found it interesting, rather annoying, and quite perplexing that the porn industry is legal but prostitution is illegal. We love our dirty magazines out there and enjoy those tawdry films with really bad acting and close ups on male and female genitalia. Many of those people reach celebrity-type status. Totally cool with me, BUT...

In the cases of both escorting and pornographic films, people are being paid to have sex with someone; usually a stranger! As long as there is a camera capturing the action in the room and the people are being filmed while the sex is happening, it is considered "art" and therefore legal to be paid. Yet an exchange of money between two consenting adults who want to have a private sexual encounter is deemed illegal. It makes absolutely no sense to me and never has!

The majority of the people who participate in the escorting industry, whether it be the ladies who are sex providers or gentlemen seeking them, are wonderful souls. I met fabulous people who were smart, savvy, and successful! I only had one terrible experience in three and a half years. There were a few "dud" clients but understandably not everyone has perfect chemistry. I always tried to find the positive in each appointment even if it fell back on that little envelope that I knew was waiting for me on the bedside table. That white envelope was enough to approach each session with excellence!

Sometimes Ya Gotta Take the Bad With the Good

There were some things that I really didn't enjoy about escorting.

My number one pet peeve was a man's smelly balls! Yes, you read that correctly. Why a man would even think that a woman would want to go anywhere near such atrocities, I'll never get! Seriously people, a few minutes of shaving "the area", sudsing up a couple of times and washing your balls so they're nice and clean is not that difficult!

NOTE: In a relationship where a wife or girlfriend doesn't want to go down on you, you might want to analyze your hygiene". Also... IF you are uncircumcised, pull that foreskin back and wash and wash it again!

**Ladies; The same goes for us! Washing that cha cha (your vagina) is imperative as well. It works both ways for intimacy to be successful for couples.

Lack of antiperspirant was another simple thing that could have been avoided just by keeping some in a carry bag or glove compartment in a car. If it was real bad, I would suggest a shower if the gent didn't do so on his own. Body odor is gross and is super easy to remedy if one cares enough. I always had antiperspirant spray for my gents convenience along with lots of other hygiene products.

Cigarette, cigar, or even the occasional pot smokers were never enjoyable for me since I was not a smoker of any substance. For your information: A smoker's semen tastes terribly bitter and nasty (There are ways to help this).

One other aspect of my escorting days that I wasn't fond of was being treated like I was a robotic sex machine from a few clients here and there. I always felt it was rather rude. I was known for my exceptional oral skills so at times I would attract the men who I think had me confused with their vacuum cleaner hose! I was not an electronic device with its own suction motor. I actually needed to come up for air every once in a while! I know I was being paid, and I understood them wanting to get their money's worth, but I always prided myself in being quite generous with my time for "satisfaction's sake".

Speaking of time, having to be a clock-watcher because a gent would try to be sly and stay for longer than the paid for time was infuriating. If my schedule allowed, I would be generous and let the gent stay past his allotted time, but also felt it was disrespectful to assume that they could just stay without asking. Especially without offering a little something for the extra time. Having to ask the man to leave, well, that never should have to be a decision a lady has to make. Common sense is a great quality to have and use.

Ewwww That Smell

One lovely afternoon I was having what I would consider to be a standard bread and butter session; The guys who would make an hour appointment in the late afternoon to get whatever they weren't getting at home, before they went home. No depth to the conversation if there was even much conversation at all! It was usually more like, "Wham bam, thank you ma'am!" This particular guy was there because he had heard about me and read of my fabulous different skills.

He was of course, lying on his back while I was doing my thing, trying to work my magic on him. He began to squirm and I could feel his butt cheeks tighten as he tensed up when suddenly as my mouth is wrapped around his "manhood", I smelled the nastiest gas I had ever smelled in my life! This guy, while I had my head in his crotch, had the audacity to pass the biggest *silent but deadly* gas ever!

My sweet little kitty cat "Boo Boo Beatrice" was in the room sleeping and the poor thing woke up and started sneezing and running around back and forth and then tried to get out the door.

I grew up with the kind of dad who loved to ask us to pull his finger or do the wind up with his arm and point his finger at one of us kids as we'd franticly duck and run for cover because we knew that dad had a big ol' fart coming someone's way... But dear ol' dad always pre warned us. This guy didn't warn me at all!

Of course, the smell lingered (for what seemed to be forever) and the guy excused himself from the room as I'm sure he wanted to get out of my place as soon as he could out of sheer humiliation. I didn't say a word to him after that except goodbye and as soon as he left I opened up all the windows and doors and fumigated my bedroom and then threw my bedding in the washer. I was disgusted at the fact that he didn't even apologize or acknowledge what he had done, but then knowing he practically caused my cat to go blind from the vapors was enough for him to perhaps die of embarrassment. Well that and the fact that his SBD fart story is now immortalized in non-fiction print!

I Literally Could Have Died

(Disclaimer: The following chapter contains graphic details. Squeamish readers beware!)

One time I ended up in the hospital due to a client hurting me. I strongly believe it was God's protection that saved me while I was being dumped off at the NW Hospital emergency doors while bleeding profusely from my vagina.

It was the last evening of "work" before I was hopping a plane to fly east to Marblehead, Massachusetts for personal travel, as myself, rather than "Kendra", to meet a very amazing guy whom I had got to know via a social dating website. He was funny, smart, and a perfect combination of all of the cool things I like in a guy; He was a firefighter who had long hair (small towns are more lenient on guys hair length, I guess).

I actually wasn't supposed to be working, but Caryssa called late in the afternoon begging me to take some appointments like a little kid would plead to their parents for a new toy. She had three men lined up for me that night which equated to about $750 for me after her cut. Of course the money would come in handy for my trip, so I agreed to take the clients!

After I rushed to get ready for my evening, I headed out the door into what was horrible rain, even by Seattle's standards. I ran to the car in my high heels. I was glad that I had worn pants and a top instead of a dress because it was chilly as well as wet. When I got to the freeway, traffic on the interstate was disastrous! I remember something inside of me saying, "Probably should call Caryssa and tell her it's not worth trying to get up north" and I had a feeling that I shouldn't go. I and told her I was definitely going to be late to my first appointment, but I *didn't* tell her I had a strange gut feeling about it. She told me not to stress, and just wanted me to get there safely, so I continued on up north toward to the place where the client was waiting.

I decided to get off the freeway and head up the back roads thinking it would be faster. I went some crazy round-about way and called Caryssa again to tell her I had somehow gotten lost, but I knew I was close to where I needed to be. She said something to the effect of maybe it's not worth it to go see this guy since he was a last minute client anyway. I asked her if he was cool and did he check out on her background search of him and she said he did, so I said, "I can go; I'll just get in there do my thing, make him happy, get my money and be on my way to the others". She laughed and said okay and we hung up.

When I got to the motel room, I knocked on the door. It was promptly opened by a handsome enough man with blue eyes and yellow-blonde stiffly sprayed hair. He looked like a stocky middle-aged Ken doll. His name was Jack. He seemed excited, a bit hyper but he was pleasant. The TV was on and it had porn playing which I thought to myself, "Oh great, he wants me to play "porn star", which always entailed a bit of weird acrobatics unlike my usual standard of service. The more he talked the more uneasy I felt so I just proceeded to get him to the bed so I could hopefully use my "Kendra" charm on him and drag out my playfulness with a bit of teasing and then a quick sex romp and we'd be done! He was acting strange, quite jittery like maybe he was on coke or something. He said, "C'mon baby. Take off your clothes and lay down with your legs open. I wanna look at that beautiful p---y of yours". Unenthusiastically, I obliged him and he began to touch me and probe a bit with his fingers. He had a large bottle of "lube" and he was drenching my vagina with it. Then he put his fingers inside and kept talking about how awesome my p---y was and how he wished he could climb up inside because it was so beautiful (Weird thing to say to me, but I've heard stranger things). He was laying across my lower abdomen with his back toward me so I couldn't really see him probing, I could only feel what was going on.

By this point I had mentally gone into my "zone out" place to get through the remainder of the hour. It was the best way I knew how to get through any uncomfortable sexual situation; a defense mechanism of sorts. That's usually what I had done all my life up to that point with any sexual encounter that I wasn't finding to be anywhere near enjoyable. Something I learned to do as a young girl when I was being sexually molested was to disconnect my mind from my body and go to a happy place instead.

After what I think was a few minutes of my "escape to fantasy-land", I felt excruciating pain like a "punch" inside my vagina but I felt it more like up in my stomach. Instantly I POPPED back to reality. I cried out, "Oh my gosh! What are you doing? It hurts really bad". He wickedly started laughing and joyfully exclaimed through his laughter, "Oh man, this is cool, you are so effing cool! My fist is all the way up inside of you and it's what I've wanted to do to somebody since I read an article about fisting and saw pictures of it!"

I said to him (trying not to freak out), "Get it out of me!! I don't do that!! You need to seriously ask a girl before you just shove your fist up her"!! He said he figured it would be okay since I get paid to have sex with him". To which with gritted teeth, I sternly said, "I get paid for my time and companionship. If I choose to have sex with you it's my choice, not your command! This isn't sex! This is NOT what I'm into! Get your fist out of me!"

By this time I just wanted to get out of there. As Jack removed his fist from me, I felt a suctioned pull from the force as it came out. I immediately put my fingers down to my vagina and asked him if I was bleeding. He said, "No," then had the audacity to try and mount me for sex after that! I told him to get off of me because by that point I was pissed off and wanted out!

There was a bit of blood on my fingers, so I told him I needed to go clean up. I got up and stood beside the bed. Suddenly I felt warm liquid running down my leg. I looked down and saw blood rushing down the inside of my legs... A LOT of blood! Up to that point I had tried not to panic, staying in control of the situation. I hurried to the bathroom and got into the shower and the water was bloody like a horror film would be. I knew I was hurt to the point of needing to get to the hospital since blood was gushing out of me and I was growing faint. I told him I needed my phone and that I was going to call Caryssa. He started to panic but gave me the phone. I called her and told her what had happened and that I was hurt and needed either an ambulance or him to get me to a hospital. She told me to put him on the phone and then she went ballistic on him screaming with a huge amount of F-word expletives while threatening that she would "ruin him" if he didn't get me to the hospital immediately!

By this time, I had bloodied all but a bath and a hand towel in the hotel room. He told me to get my stuff and hurry up. He didn't have to tell me twice!! I knew if we didn't hurry it could get critical for me. All I could think of was my kids and how I needed to be strong and stay alive for them. I placed the bath towel like a diaper between my legs and put my pants on over it. Luckily the pants that I'd worn happened to have some stretch to them and held the towels perfectly in place!

Before we left the room, I made sure to grab my well-deserved money envelope from the douchebag after Caryssa reminded me to do so. I climbed into his car and laid down as he started to drive just thinking, "Stay awake, stay awake, your kids need you to live". I had thoughts of what people would think if they heard I died like this, especially those who had no clue of my career choice, which was nearly everybody I knew. For some reason I thought about my firefighter friends; Mostly because besides Helga, they were my dearest friends at that time in my life. I didn't want them to find out about how stupid I was to allow this to happen to me! I guess I should have listened to that "inner voice" earlier when I had so much trouble even getting up to the appointment.

I tried to stay awake but I was feeling weaker. I began to pray and ask Jesus to help me to be alright and get me in safely where they could help me. By the time we got to the hospital, I was dizzy, delirious, and feeling very faint. I remember Jack pulling on me to get me out of the car onto the sidewalk. Then he ran around to his side of the car, jumped in the driver's seat and drove away. He left me standing there dumped off in the rain on the curb outside of the hospital emergency entrance.

I have no other explanation as to how I got inside of the emergency room, to where I was able to tell the triage nurse what was happening to me, other than God's mighty hand carrying me. Jesus promises that He will always be there for us no matter what and He means it! All of a sudden, I was inside at the desk of emergency. I'm guessing I was pretty pale by that point. They immediately grabbed a wheelchair and asked what was wrong. I told them I was bleeding from my vagina and I thought I was going to pass out. I heard them say "Stay with us," and then I woke up in a bed in emergency with my legs up in the stirrups and the doctor was stitching me up inside of my vagina, which now that I look back, it is impressive how they can get up inside of there and fix a wound like that!

I could have and perhaps should have died that night I was injured by Jack. I lost quite a bit of blood; They figured it was at least two pints by the way I had been bleeding when I got there and by the timeline I had told them about afterward when I came to. It took nine stitches inside my vaginal walls for the gash to be sewn shut so the bleeding would stop. I was fortunate that the damage wasn't worse. For what had been done to me that night, my attending gynecologist told me that others have died from that same sex act. I was lucky, she said, that I had given birth three times so my body was able to handle how Jack had injured me. They asked me if I wanted the police called and of course like any smart call girl, hooker, or any kind of "prostitute" who isn't protected by any laws, I said, "No thank you!"

That was the only really bad moment in my three and a half years as an escort. God's word tells us that "He will never leave us or forsake us." It doesn't matter what you do, what you say, think, or feel. He willingly forgives you over and over if you just ask. I've walked away from Him so many times in my life, but He is patient and just sits, quietly waiting. He loves us and meets us right where we're at even if that is while bleeding profusely because of an injury from having sex with a stranger for money.

I feel that God would prefer that our relationship with Him would remain more consistent rather than regularly walking away. Life is much more victorious with Him in the driver's seat. At least this has been my experience. My point here is that even in the midst of Jack's harmful sex act on me, God watched over me that night, and it wasn't conditional on if I was walking obediently next to Him according to "The Bible," but in fact it was because He simply loves me. That is my perspective.

With my optimistic attitude, I find that the good always outweighs the bad. During my escorting career, allow me to emphasize that I had some really good clients. Many of them exceeded my expectations that I had prior to actually doing this for a living. The majority of the men I was fortunate to meet and spend time with were very classy, down to earth and all around great gentlemen. I'd say 99% of them "Get it" when it comes to how to treat a woman!

Some might ask why I feel I needed to tell such a vivid recollection of the trauma of that evening. After all it really is too much information. I say, "No it's not too much information, because I'm lucky to be here to tell others what can happen to thousands of girls (and guys) out there on any given day. When they knock on a new client's door, then step inside and the door shuts behind them, there is always a slight chance that danger of some kind could be in store.

I also want those who might be quick to judge to understand that we have no right to judge others! Simply put, It is our responsibility to love others. If you have a problem with that, then that's completely on you. To show kindness, compassion, and understanding for people in the sex industry, rather than look down your noses at them like they are trash could be a turning point for those who might not have anyone else willing to show them grace!

As for my trip to Marblehead, that I was preparing to take, prior to that awful meeting with Jack, I did get to go. JP (the firefighter) was a wonderful host. We had a fabulous weekend sightseeing around Salem, Gloucester, and of course Marblehead. We never saw each other after that weekend. I guess I wasn't his "it girl". About a year after that weekend a friend of his told me he is "afraid of a second date". At least I got to meet a really cool person and see some fun sights out of the first date!

Toys, Trinkets, Treats, and Treasures

Besides being paid for my time spent with men, I would often receive lovely gifts from my clients. Some of the tokens of appreciation I received were lingerie sets, oils and lotions and spa or salon visits. I also was given gift cards to my favorite stores like Target (Who doesn't enjoy spending money there?) or The Disney Store (I was a collector of Disney art). I received countless bottles of wine and craft beers. My favorite wine was one that I later found to be $375 a bottle (So happy that I savored that one)! We used to get fresh copper river salmon from someone a few times during the run each year.

Delicious chocolates were given to me as well. I received concert or theatre tickets, Disney collectibles, my favorite fragrance which is still "Pure Poison" by Dior, exquisite floral bouquets, dresses, troy ounces of silver, artisan Italian beaded necklaces, a rich red leather-bound journaling book (which I used to make notes for this book), as well as a very old copy of "Alice's Adventures in Wonderland." I received various CD's because everyone knew how much I love music, especially late 70's and all 80's rock! The list goes on of the material generosities by the men I met.

The majority of my guys were thoughtful people. Sometimes they would even bring gifts for Brittnee or the boys. One very cool cat gave my boys their first Xbox! Another friend made sure my boys had the shoes they needed for sports. My daughter received gift cards to different stores from time to time so she could get clothing and fun things she wanted.

Many of the men I met up with had such caring and compassionate hearts. They genuinely showed interest in my life and my kids' lives as well. Those men who I saw on a weekly or regular basis would keep up on how my boys' baseball or football teams were doing. They'd ask about my daughter and her high school plays. One client even came to watch one of her plays because after hearing me talk about the show he thought it sounded interesting.

Because MILF's were popular at the time, I was fortunate to draw in the young men; The twenty-something crowd. They wanted to be taught some things and also wanted to experience sexual encounters without having to play the head-games that came along with the young women hoping for a permanent relationship. I was the perfect candidate for them!

Many of the more mature escorts I knew wouldn't see the younger guys. Some had boys of their own in college so that was too weird for them. Others didn't appreciate the "energy level" of the youngsters. For some, the appointments would be referenced, booked and set for young men all to find that they would end up as a "no show", resulting in lost revenue for that day.

I had no problem seeing those young men. Some of my favorite clients were in that 20-something age group. Several of them were college students and very intelligent; Smarter than I was by far! I may have had life experience, but these guys were book-smart and tech savvy.

I often wonder where some of them landed in life. I did receive emails over the years from a few of them. They each in their own way updated me on their lives, letting me know that they were married and had little babies. They thanked me for teaching them not only about sex, but also about being a good lover, an attentive husband, and how to be a present parent in their children's lives. Knowing that I had a positive influence and impact on their lives in some small way is a good feeling.

Their Secret's Safe
With Me

Over the years I've been asked several times if I ever met with any high-profile people like celebrities, billionaires or the like. I always give the same answer: "I'll never tell!" What's the point? It serves me no personal gain to tell who ANY of my clients were. For many, they stand to lose much if I make their names public. I don't have a "little black book." I never kept one. I had lots of random pieces of paper, sticky notes, and a few scribbled names on junk mail envelopes. I saw no reason to keep records of names. I always planned that if I got busted, I would never tell names of gents just to get myself out of trouble. Why take somebody else's life down with yours? That's not my style.

I have many fond memories with most all of the gents I encountered. To me they are all rock stars because they kept me and my kids housed in a very beautiful home in a great community and allowed me to be able to stay available and present for my three kids in the years they needed me the most! I'm grateful to every single one of the men who sought me out to spend time with me. I made great memories with the majority of them! However, it was a business and I treated it as such. These people were human beings with private lives and they didn't need me to mess in their personal affairs with hopes of any personal gain!

Who are these men that seek out willing women that accept cash in return for time, companionship and uninhibited sexual play? These men I met came from all walks of life! They were smart, funny, interesting, playful, romantic, spontaneous, successful, kind, and sweet. I liked them! There were "Average Joe's, blue collar workers, creative artists, computer geeks (God bless the dot com generation of that time). There were professionals in white collar careers, multi-millionaires and also those who had to tuck money away and save it just to see me from time to time. Some worked "for the man" while others ran their own businesses, and there were even military men (who by the way did receive a military discount)! Some were religious, others not so much. I spent time with Atheists, Christians, Jews, Buddhists, Hindu, Catholics, and probably other religions. I didn't usually survey my clients, but many times God became a topic of "small talk" with them as we lay there chatting. There were various political affiliations and one who even looked and sounded like a former president (truly uncanny), but definitely was not!

Most of my clients were what I classify as average in looks. Just regular guys. Fairly short to incredibly tall in stature. Some were thin while others were chubby or fat. I saw men of different ethnic backgrounds. There were a few international clients as well. Many of the men I met were decently muscular. A few were practically too hot for me to handle and I'm able to handle a lot of hotness! There were guys nearly old enough to be high school chums with my dad and others were the perfect age for me to date had I been in dating mode and they available to do so.

The younger 20-somethings and 30-somethings always boosted my ego! Some clients I only met once and many I saw so often that if I ran into them today, I would simply introduce them as a longtime friend of mine. They were your neighbors, friends, and coworkers; figuratively speaking. The guy you see at the grocery store or bump into in line at the local deli counter could be a former client of mine. They could be anybody you might encounter on any given day.

Clients of escorts are regular normal people!

As I keep mentioning, I had some wonderful men that I had the opportunity to meet with. There are so many memories of the usual fun sexual encounters, but there is so much more depth beyond that which I had the pleasure of experiencing. I developed trustworthy relationships with the people I met with throughout each week. When a man is giving you his personal information; enough info that you could take it and tear his world apart, but instead you guard and protect it, that builds trust. When you allow a stranger into your home, inviting him into your bedroom, where anything can happen, that builds trust as well. Going to a man's home also brings complete vulnerability as you have no idea what awaits you. You hope all of your homework in checking good solid references by others who have encountered him before or your personal information you've gathered from him checks out in your people search! You and the gentleman enter into a non-verbal unspoken agreement to protect each other's privacy.

Over the years I've shared non-incriminating things with my daughter and her friends as well as my friends about some of the gentlemen I've met. Being careful to not reveal my clients is very important to me. My ability to share some of the situations or scenarios with people I feel helps them to better understand what really goes on during these encounters beyond the possibilities of sex happening. Some of the stories I've told them are about normal life things that happen to my clients, other stories share an awkward or sad moment. I also have a few funny stories I've shared.

I could share a little bit about nearly every man I met because I do remember almost every one. By face for sure I do; Some of the names have slipped away over time, and I suppose many of them have probably forgotten me as well... As it should be!

Keeping in mind of course that all names have been changed to protect the identities of my beloved clients, I have decided that several of these stories just need to be shared for clearer insight and fresh perspective on this secret misunderstood activity of escort encounters.

Johnny Q

One Saturday afternoon shortly after I began my solo career as Sandhal, I received a phone call from a prospective new client. He was wondering if I would be able to meet with him at his house sometime early in the upcoming week. I asked him his name, if he had references, and if he could tell me where he lived. He said his name was Johnny Q, then gave me his references and let me know he lived a bit further out and so most girls don't like to visit him. When he told me where he lived I said that wouldn't be a problem if he would throw in extra cash for my travel time. He agreed and thought that was fair. I told him I would check his references and let him know once I heard back from the ladies which might take a few days especially since it was the weekend and many girls didn't work on weekends.

I got replies from the few ladies he gave me for references and I phoned him to say we were good to go and what day and time would he like me to visit him. We agreed on a day early in the week and an early afternoon time so I would hopefully not end up getting stuck in rush hour traffic on the way back to my place in the city. He asked me if I had stockings to bring along and I told him I did. Then he asked me what colors they were and I told him they were the usual tones like nude, beige, and black. With a sigh of disappointment, he said, "Okay." I asked him what colors he was hoping for and he replied that he likes colorful stockings like pink, green, yellow and red. I snickered a bit and said I could try and get some before we met and he said okay. Over the weekend I didn't have a chance to go to a mall or many stores. I could only find some white and navy blue stockings, but I bought them for my meet up with Johnny Q.

He called the evening before to confirm the appointment for the next day, which is standard etiquette for clients to do with escorts so they don't lose out on potential money making for a day. At that I told him I was unable to find bright colored stockings, but I would bring every pair along that I had. He seemed happy with that information.

The next day I called him to let him know I was on my way to his place and I'd be there in about an hour or so. He told me that when I got to his place that it would be okay to let myself in because he might be in the middle of doing something. I let him know I could let myself in just fine then if it would be helpful for him. "That would be great," he said and then he asked me to call him when I got close to his place. I arrived in the area a little earlier than expected, but didn't know exactly where his place was, so I called and said I was close by. His voice was a bit muffled but I could hear him enough to tell me that I could just drive down the alley park in the back of the house in the gravel parking area.

About 10 minutes later I turned down the alley where his older two-story farm-style house was and I parked in the gravel lot. I started to gather my little Sandhal bag that held my variety of condoms, lube, and other things along with my purse when my phone rang. It was Johnny telling me that once I get inside to come up to the attic where he was at. I reluctantly said okay and proceeded to walk up to the back door of the house and opened the door...

This is the part in the scary movie where we all start to yell at the movie screen and tell the stupid girl to turn around and run, and I possibly should have! My curiosity was piqued by this time because this guy who first requested brightly colored stockings and now couldn't greet me at his door was in this house, up in the attic and I was about to go in and find him... How could I leave now? Besides it was broad daylight and rarely do bad things happen in movies until night falls!

I walked in through the creaky door that led me into the kitchen. It was basically styled after an old mid-western farm house. The house was absolutely silent except the clicking of my heels as I walked across the kitchen floor. Straight ahead of me was the living room, filled with antique furniture and decor. I called out, "Hello! --- Hello?" to which there was no reply. Now that I was far enough inside the house, I noticed it was completely silent except for the ticking of the grandfather clock's pendulum that I could hear coming from the living room. Suddenly it began to chime the standard tune of all clocks at the top of the hour. It was such an epically eerie moment! As the clock struck the hour I turned right down a hallway where I could see some rooms ahead. I kept calling hello, but never heard an answer back. I finally found a steep stairway leading up so I stepped up the creaky stairs.

Once I reached the top there was a landing where I saw a room at one end and a small set of three stairs leading into what must have been the attic! I turned and faced it and called out another, "Hello?" I faintly heard a muffled, "I'm up here," from the room at the top of those few stairs. As I was walking up, I could hear what seemed to be a kind of grunting and just as I stepped inside, there was Johnny Q, built like an offensive lineman, sitting in a chair, beating off, wearing a granny-style green one-piece bathing suit and covered completely from head to toe in stockings. The only part of his body that had bare skin showing was his penis! He was rocking back and forth grunting from his sexual arousal as he was stroking himself. He had a white pair of stockings pulled over his head and face so he looked like a wacky combination of the Trix Rabbit meets "old school" robber!!

I stood there for a moment, stunned and speechless. He suddenly said, "I've been a very bad boy. I'm a really bad boy and I need to be punished." I was motionless for about 10 to 15 seconds and then burst into laughter! I had no clue what to do at that point. I wasn't one of those role-playing girls and even if I was, I would have needed a little forewarning of this scenario. Instead, I walked naively right into that house, up the stairs and experienced one of the most interesting and hilarious sights I've ever happened upon!

I told him, as I was desperately trying to stifle my laughter, that I wasn't "that kind of girl" and without missing a beat he said, "Well, I've been a very bad boy and I need you to punish me. Maybe you should drag me across the floor."

Oh Lordy! I had to decide really quick what my next move was. Either I just stop him right there and say thanks but no thanks, or I just go with it and see what transpires. Of course I decided to just play along and go with the flow!

I pulled on him by some of the hosiery around his neck and shoulders as I told him he was a very bad boy and that I was going to have to discipline him. He got down off the chair onto his hands and knees and began willingly crawling across the floor as I pretended to drag him. He crawled down the hallway into what I guess was his room in his parents' house..

The "activity" between us that afternoon was minimal at best. Mostly he liked and wanted to be degraded. Of course, me being curious and bold enough to ask, I wanted to know if he had any memory of being sexually molested as a child and he said hadn't. I asked him what the fascination with being mummified in stockings was all about and he told me he remembers as a child, he was bare naked, playing in a clothes basket and there were stockings in there. He said they rubbed up against him and he got his first memorable erection. Ever since, his excitement level gets amped up when he's covered in stockings!

I only got to see him a couple of times as Sandhal. Of course I saw him again after that first day! How could I not after the first experience being so fabulous for storytelling?

The next time I saw him was at night. Since I had already seen him, I knew he was safe and I was actually super excited to see him. He was my only "novelty client" with an intriguing fetish!

Of course, he asked me to bring some stockings for our 2nd meeting, which I thought was sort of funny since the first time around he obviously had plenty of his own! I brought along a few brand new pairs that I had purchased just to give to him for his collection. I also brought some of my own.

He called me prior to our appointment before I got to the house and asked if I could stop at a store to pick up a cake for us. Cake? Of course I said yes I would I oblige him. Who wouldn't want a sexual encounter with a dessert of cake included?! The store I went to didn't have much of a selection so I chose a white frosted cake with raspberry custard filling. It was a typical layered cake with yellow flowers and green leaves. It looked and smelled delicious!

Johnny asked me to meet him at different house than our first meeting place was at. I think the second meeting might have been his aunt's house or some other family member. This house was very late seventies mixed with early eighties in style and decor. When I got there, of course like the first time, I did have to let myself in. This time I didn't hesitate to play "hide and go seek" with Johnny Q! I was mentally prepared far better this time around since I knew somewhat what to expect.

I walked into the house, this time through the front door and right into the living room. Straight ahead was the dining room leading into the kitchen. I walked in and set the cake down on the table in the dining room and proceeded down the hallway calling out to Johnny. I heard the familiar muffled noises coming from the room at the end of the hallway. I walked into the dimly lit room where there was a queen size four poster canopy bed! Right smack dab in the middle, resting against the headboard was my favorite stocking mummy covered from head to toe including that hilarious "bunny gone bad" look again! This time he was wearing a pastel colored lacy piece of lingerie over his stocking clad body instead of granny's green bather! Of course his penis was out and erect while he was grunting and stroking. I immediately told him he was a very bad boy and since he was naughty I would have to punish him. He told me he was the bride and needed to be dressed for the wedding and needed my help first before I punished him. Mind you, he's the size of a linebacker.

He told me to go to the drawers where his wedding attire was kept. I opened up the drawer which was filled with big old styled bras with thick back-straps that were not even remotely sexy! There were also a few lacy cover-ups and several pairs of granny panties. I picked out a few things and asked if they were his wedding clothes and he enthusiastically said they were! So, like any good wedding attendant would, I helped him get ready for his "wedding night."

Of course, me being me, I told him that one day I was going to write a book about my life as

Sandhal and I asked him if he would mind me telling of my encounters with him. He popped out of character long enough to say he would be happy if I talked about him and he was super excited to know he would someday be in my book! He even posed for some pictures on my flip-phone, but sadly much to my dismay, that phone died and over time I ended my cell phone account that had all the pictures saved online. I suppose some tech wizard could find them, but alas you must use your imagination to visualize the now legendary Johnny Q!

After I got Johnny dressed and ready for his moment, it was time to drag him down the "aisle" or the hallway as most people call it! I'm a very detail oriented person and I had done lots of event planning in the past including weddings. The bride must always have a song to go down the aisle to, so I hummed "The Wedding March!"

While being "dragged" down the hallway on his hands and knees he told me it was time for the reception and asked me if the wedding cake was there. Lightbulb! It wasn't a cake for dessert that I was sent to the store to get, it was a cake for a fantasy prop. I told him the cake was on the table. Johnny crawled over to it and swiped the frosting with his finger. He looked up at me with that nylon covered face of his and said he was a bad boy for touching the cake and needed punishment. I told him I would punish him alright and he said he should be punished for eating the frosting by me shoving the cake in his face!

Bonus round for the call girl! I was getting paid to play this fun little twisted game where I would get to shove an entire cake in his face!

Of course, as usual, I started laughing because the sight before me was ridiculously awesome; this big burly young man, covered in nylons, elastic, and lace was on his knees begging for me to shove a cake in his face. He said he needed to take his veil off and pulled the white pantyhose off of his face.

I picked up the cake and held it in my left hand and proceeded to walk over to him. I stood over him and sternly told him how bad of a boy he had been for eating the frosting. I said to him, "Since you wanted this cake so much that you couldn't wait for everyone to have some, then I'll give you the whole cake!", and then I shoved and smooshed that cake into Johnny's face. It was fabulous!

Lying on the floor, with his frosting covered face, he told me to undress so he could share the cake with me. Suffice to say I ended up that night getting frosting in places I never imagined you could frost!

After that night, Johnny Q and I tried to meet up again but our schedules never seemed to work out. I did talk with him one afternoon a few years ago by phone. He was calling from inside of his closet. He was grunting... He told me that he recently got married, but his wife has no clue about his secret desire to be mummified in stockings. He was hoping I could see him because he had no other outlet for his needs to be fulfilled. He really didn't want anything sexual. For him it was about being mummified and humiliated. I wish I could have helped him, but I couldn't get up to his location from where I live now.

It's harmless fantasy play that Johnny likes to experience and I encouraged him to share it with his wife. He believes she wouldn't understand. It makes me sad that there are so many people out there like Johnny who just need that outlet where they can play pretend and fulfill their desires, yet they can't share their intimate secrets because their partners are unwilling or too uptight or would think it's freaky or uncomfortable. That is one reason why there will always be a need for girls like me!

Darren

As "Kendra" I didn't choose which clients I would get in an evening. Caryssa would get the requests and send me out to meet the gentlemen. One Friday evening she sent me out somewhere around town for my first appointment. I was occupied for a couple of hours with that first guy. After two hour dude was done she sent me out to an area known as the east side.

I was sent to a hotel in the area where a younger more handsome man was waiting for me. His name was Darren. He was quite tall, slim build but not super skinny. He had chestnut brown longer hair and a chiseled jawline. Actually, he was what I would consider to be my type if I was dating and had been in my early thirties rather than my early forties and not been being paid to be there! When I tried to make small talk, Darren didn't offer much back to me. I always liked to try and get to know a bit about a guy I hadn't met before rather than just walking into a room, stripping down to my naked self, and proceeding to just have sex with him.

That's kind of what ended up happening at first though since he seemed to be tense and quiet, I just figured he had a bad day, maybe got in a fight at home and needed to blow off some steam. I unbuttoned his shirt and began to explore his body and we quickly ended up on the bed. Then out of nowhere he starts chatting it up with me and asking me all sorts of things about me, my work, if I like it, was I married or single. I told him I had three kids and shared with him that I was escorting because I make good enough money to not have to work a lot and therefore am able to be there for my kids easier than if I had regular average jobs.

After a few minutes of chatting he excused himself to go to the restroom. I could see as he got up that he had an huge erection so I was a bit more at ease knowing that at least he was a bit turned on. I laid back on the bed and went to reach for my little "bag of condoms" and accidentally knocked in the floor. I was feeling giddy and gleefully turned to reach down to grab the bag and bonked my head hard into the corner of the nightstand. Oh it hurt! I put my hand to my head and it felt wet. I had broken my head open. Not badly, but when a person breaks their head open, usually the blood pours out quickly making it look much worse than what it really is.

I frantically tried to get the blood to stop, but when I looked in the mirror attached to the dresser which was right next to my side of the bed, I saw half my face dripping in blood as well as falling down from my hand to my arm. That is when Darren rounded the corner having come from the bathroom. The look on his face was of horror and panic! I was nervously laughing because I knew it was far worse than what it looked like but I could tell that he was freaked out. I told him about my little mishap trying to pick up my little bag of goodies for our playtime. He didn't find it to be as funny as I did. He did go grab a washcloth for me and made sure I was okay. I excused myself to go clean up and I put a band aid on my head which, by the way is a super attractive look that's very sexy for an escort!

He calmed down long enough for us to have about a 10 minute sex-session; enough for him to get his rocks off and then he got dressed faster than I've seen anyone do so before! He left my envelope on the dresser along with those luscious cookies that certain hotels have waiting for you in their rooms! The "hour-long" appointment with Darren lasted for about 25 minutes. I got my full hourly rate and the cookies! I called Caryssa and told her I'd meet up with her for her "cut" and a cookie... While we ate the cookies, I told her what happened and after we finished laughing at my replay of the "bonk on the head", she told me the guy was married and literally lived right up the street from the hotel. He was probably freaking in his boots at the fact that I could have hurt myself worse. The room was in his name and his world could have crashed down around him. She said maybe it would help scare him into getting his act together and work on his marriage. Needless to say, Darren was a one-time client for me!

Sam

Some people have a way of touching your life and making you feel like the only one in the world that matters. That's how it was with Sam every time we met.

Our sessions had to take place in the late morning or early afternoon for discretionary purposes. I would drive to his beautiful east side home in an upper class neighborhood on a quiet cul de sac. He would always be waiting for me at his front door with it open and ready to swoop me inside for our little secret rendezvous. He would shut the door and embrace me, holding me tightly as though he never wanted to leave. A bottle of chilled dry champagne and two glasses set and ready for us to toast our time together was a staple for each illicit meeting. Even though I would choose some pretty little something to wear under my dresses for his viewing pleasure, he would most always have some type of lingerie draped over a chair waiting for me to slip into. There were mirrors everywhere. We usually began our trysts in his sitting parlor. There were mirrors propped up on tables, on the floor and on whatever pieces of furniture we weren't sitting on.

We would kiss and touch and caress and just gaze into each other's eyes like a couple in love. He craved that kind of affection. It was easy for me to respond to him because he had a cool Kiefer Sutherland-type look that I was highly attracted to. Sam completely intrigued me and I knew outside of my Sandhal world if we had met, we would have clicked. We had great chemistry! He "got" me and I "got" him as well.

After we had fun in the parlor, we would go up to a guest room in the house. I always liked it when I knew a man was married and he didn't take me to his actual bedroom. It told me that he truly loved his wife even though there was something lacking in their intimacy.

When we arrived to the guest room there were mirrors set up all over the place just like they were downstairs. They owned a lot of mirrors! He loved to watch our activity from every angle. This is where a lady really needs to be comfortable in her skin because every inch of it could be seen from every angle all around the room!

One of my favorite things he would say to me after the first time we met, each time thereafter when we spent time together was, "You came back!" He would say it like I was a long-lost love of his that he thought he had lost forever. It was sweet.

I remember one time while we were together he asked me to come stay with him for a weekend at his cabin. I had to politely decline because I didn't feel like I could leave my kids home for a few days while I drove to some unreachable cabin in the woods though it would have been lovely. I sensed that his feelings about me were growing stronger. I began to realize that he was feeling a deeper affection toward me than just a hired girl there to please him. I remember him expressing once that if he had the money he would pay me to be his exclusive lady. I definitely would have agreed to that arrangement if he would have been able to afford to keep me in that fashion.

He was a wonderful soul. I miss seeing him and hearing about his life. He shared a bit about his marriage. How his wife had gained a lot of weight after they were married. She no longer enjoyed being intimate with him because she was uncomfortable with the way she looked. He didn't strike me as the type of guy who cared one way or the other about weight gain. He just had a desire to be 100% into the person he was with and he adored every inch of her no matter what. I know this because I was certainly not a hard body. I had a baby tummy from having three kids. My middle aged boobs were not implants and gravity shows no mercy! I also had cellulite and other imperfections on my body. He never once complained nor did he tell me to leave because I wasn't perfect. He accepted me as I was, and I'm certain he did so with his wife as well. Sadly she had insecurities and self-esteem issues to the point of allowing their intimacy to dwindle down to none at all.

One time Sam expressed that he loved me. It kind of freaked me out. I know there were intense feelings between us, but I tried never to cross the line between being a professional and allowing it to get personal. I have many fond memories of Sam. I know he could find me if he ever wished to do so, because he found me once when he had lost track of me, through someone we both know outside of my Sandhalworld! I never say never, so I could see him again someday...

White Envelopes

Stig

My Sandhal presentation to the escorting community in Seattle was playfully witty, mixed with articulate finesse. I attracted men accordingly. I didn't command the highest hourly rates out there, but I could hold my own even as one of the most mature providers in the Seattle area. As a forty-one year old woman I presented and carried myself with class and refinement, yet I remained approachable and playful for prospective clients.

When I first met Stig, I think I was living in my penthouse overlooking the Lake just north of downtown. I remember meeting him and thinking, "Dang, I hit the jackpot with this one!"

It was a pleasant surprise seeing this fine looking middle aged man who smelled delicious and looked like he had walked off of the cover of Forbes magazine and about to jump into my bed!

His demeanor was quiet, gentle, patient and kind. That is exactly who I still know him to be! His energy level was usually mellow and laid back. He was of medium height and build and in incredibly good shape for his age, which I believe was around my age; Maybe a bit older. I don't think I ever really asked him.

Stig was one who became a repeat client. Not a man I would see often enough to say he was a regular, but he was one who I always looked forward to hearing from. He and I built a great professional friendship! We both had kids growing up and going through school and all the things adolescents go through. We often updated each other on life at home. He opened up to me about his private life and told me things that he really couldn't share with those closest to him. It made me sad to see this man who was incredibly successful and respected in his business world have to go home to a family life that quite frankly sucked.

One thing that has always made me sad and at times even angered me, is to hear of a man who might not be "perfect", but is there and present in his family's life and married to someone who takes him; his loving care, his intimacy, his hard work, his money, and everything else he puts into his marriage and family for granted!

He was married to one of those women!

Stig and I went from being "professional associates" to honest to good friends over the years. I listened to the things he shared with me with a compassionate heart. It pained me to see how disheartened he would get over situations at home and I understood because though my life situations weren't quite the same, I too had experienced a spouse who "checked out" of our family and never once looked back at what was left in the dust.

I kept Stig and his family in prayer while they were going through some legal matters (Yes, you can pray in the midst of *sin stuff* and God will hear and answer just like any good parent will hear their child who cries out for help even if they've messed up). I watched Stig go through some tough times but he came out of them like a champ! He went through a divorce and was fortunate enough to keep his beautiful relationships with his kids intact.

Stig was fortunate a few years after his divorce to find a beautiful and talented lady and they were married and remain so. They seem so happy and that thrills me because that man is so incredibly deserving of a fulfilling marriage with a sexy woman who's gonna love him and rock his socks off as much as time allows! He got exactly what he deserved in a fantastic way.

Sk8er Boy

Before I moved into the lake view penthouse, my incall, the places I would use so gentleman could discreetly visit me, were nearby hotels just north of downtown. I had one place in particular where I made some of the fondest memories as Sandhal. I also made a few funny memories as well.

At the time, it was easiest for me to set appointments by phone. If a guy wanted to see me and had his reference phone numbers, I could usually phone the ladies to verify the references making sure the guys were safe and not LE (law enforcement), crazies, thieves, or dangerous creeps. If all went well, I'd get an appointment set for the same day or soon after.

That is how it was when I set up the time for my meeting with the guy I call "Sk8er Boy". We chatted on the phone for a while when he called me to set up the appointment. We talked about people we both knew within our little 'hobby community" as we referred to it, and we began building a little bit of rapport which was nice because it was always good to have a bit of knowledge of who I was meeting so it wasn't like having sex with a total stranger even though I was going to have sex with this stranger upon first meeting him!

During our initial phone conversation, we had shared some funny stories and laughed with each other. He actually seemed really cool and I was excited to meet him. Some of the guys who are known by several girls go by fake names too. They're able to keep their identity unknown because they have built a good solid reputation within the community, especially with the ladies. Sk8er Boy was one of those.

He was scheduled to arrive at 7pm. for his appointment with me on a lovely summertime evening. Right on time, he knocked lightly on the door. I always tried to guess what the gent was going to look like based on any information I had learned about him, by hearing his voice, or by descriptions that I might have received from a lady whom he had previously met with. What a gentleman truly looked like usually was never even close to the picture in my mind!

This time was no exception. I walked across the room to the door and opened it up. I'm guessing my mouth probably dropped or my eyes widened or both. Standing there in the hallway was an old acquaintance friend of mine from back in my school days. He was a few years older than I was. I knew him because he had dated my best friend for a little while back then.

I invited him in and I think I may have blurted out his name to which he looked completely shocked. He clearly didn't recognize me. He had only given me his fake community name... I had to explain why and how I knew him. I told him the place both he and I used to work and hangout was where we knew each other from. I told him I was a bit more nerdy back then, wore wire-framed glasses, and had much shorter hair. It made sense that at first he didn't know who I was.

I think he was a bit embarrassed that I knew him from back then and knew that he was seeing escorts around town now. What's funny about that is that I was an escort! Who was I to judge his choices in life? I was there, about to have a paid sexual encounter with him. No judgement would come from me.

Our time together that evening was nice. We had some playtime, and we had time to chat and laugh and reminisce about those good ol' days of our youth. He never contacted me again to spend time with me. I did see him out and about at some parties and functions within our little circle of companions. We would chat a bit then move on to chatting with other friends. It was probably a little too close for comfort for him, although for me, I thought it was a fun surprise to have a familiar face on the other side of the door that initial meeting day. I knew his secret would be forever safe with me.

Brendan

For many of my clients, when they first met me, they would express how pleased they were with how pretty I was. That was definitely one of my strong attributes as a provider; Having a really pretty face. That, and having great hair! Not a vain statement; Just a fact. I was blessed to have nice features that went well together! Most of the escorts like me had photos of themselves on their website so prospective clients could see what they look like, although many escorts out there hid their face from everyone for privacy purposes.

For a provider it's always a surprise when first meeting a new gentleman. Rarely would a gent send their photo to me so I could see what they looked like before we met which is understandable for their privacy, protection and discretionary purposes!

One evening I headed to an outcall appointment near the downtown area which was near where I lived. Outcalls are when a provider will go out to the home or hotel room of her client. It always made me happy when I found out my client lived close by me. There was something about some of high-rises around the city that was pretty awesome. They seemed to house some of the most handsome men of Seattle! The man I met this one particular evening definitely fell into that category!

When Brendan opened the door my heart skipped a few beats! He was absolutely gorgeous. I'd say he was most likely in his upper twenties, about six feet tall, had sandy blonde surfer hair, a nice golden tan, smoldering greyish brown eyes, and a smile that could melt Antarctica! He was nice and quite funny. A very good host that made me feel incredibly welcome and at ease right away.

I was happy that he indicated he was pleased I was there, because after my initial thrill about the escort lottery I had just won, inside I began to briefly panic! Why the heck did this guy want to see me? He was young, successful, gorgeous, and seemed to be a generally cool person. He could have his pick of any girl out there. That I was certain of! It was my brief momentary thought pattern at first, because in being "human," I have always had to fight off the "not good enough" mentality. But I was there and we seemed to have a connection.

We chatted in a very unrushed manner. He had booked plenty of time with me so it wasn't going to be a wham bam thank you ma'am session! He opened a lovely bottle of wine and we enjoyed that along with a fancy fruit and cheese tray he had delivered for our tête-à-tête! I found out he had been very successful with an online idea and had made a great amount of money doing so. He had the fortune enough to travel to his favorite cities around the world and he had stunning sculptures, paintings, and blown glass decor throughout his place that he had purchased from several places throughout

Europe. For such a young man, he certainly was living life to the fullest!

There was a mix of soft rock music playing. The wine must have given Brendan a slight buzz, enough to whisk me off the couch and whirl me around his living room, dancing to the music. At first we laughed and danced like a couple of silly kids in high school. Then he pulled me close and held me tightly. I could hear his breathing change and I felt his heart beginning to beat faster. Mine changed right along with his. It's that natural thing that occurs when two people connect and the chemistry is good. He reached his hand to my face and cupped my chin in his hand, while he gently pulled me to him for a kiss. It wasn't just any kiss. It had fire and passion. Like he had been locked away for years and finally his pent up energy was able to be released!

Brendan led me down the hallway to his bedroom never once breaking physical contact with me. The heat between us had kicked up several notches as our clothes were rapidly being thrown around the room! For the next hour or so it was all about pure unbridled sex mixed with soft sensual play. It was a beautiful occasion in his room that evening!

Even though he was very engaging and present, it seemed as though he was searching for something; like he couldn't get fulfilled. He looked deeply and passionately into my eyes several times during our private little time together. Behind the romantic gazing, I could sense a feeling that he was lost and trying to break free from something.

After we could muster absolutely no energy, we laid quietly in his big comfortably cozy bed and for quite some time neither of us spoke a word. Brendan smooched my forehead and gently whispered, "Thank you." I whispered back to him that it was my absolute pleasure and he was very welcome.

When we finally broke the silence and began a fresh conversation, I decided I was going to ask this guy as I often did, why out of all the ladies out there, did he choose me to spend his evening with? He answered simply that he liked what he had heard about me and that I seemed right for what he needed. Then out of curiosity, I asked him why he wasn't hanging out with a beautiful young woman since he could probably have his pick of any young hot twenty-something out there?

With a heavy burdened sigh, he opened up and in a shaky voice he told me that the reason he chose to see me and why he wasn't dating is because a few months prior to our meeting, he was about two weeks away from getting married to his fiancée, the love of his life, when she was involved in a freak accident and died. As he told me this, his eyes welled up and tears began rolling down his cheeks. Of course I felt terrible for bringing up the questions. Yet somehow I felt that this cleansing that was beginning to unfold was exactly what he needed to happen in order for healing of his heart to begin.

Brendan shared with me that he needed to just "be" with someone without having any possibility of a real attachment happening. Because of the things he had read or heard about me, he felt I could be exactly that person for him. He wouldn't have to worry about becoming emotionally attached because of our age difference. He knew he wasn't ready to date in the real world because of the pain he was still experiencing from the unexpected loss of his true love.

The "lost look" in his eyes suddenly made sense to me. His raw unbridled activity with me made sense as well. He had so much he was ready to give to this person whom he loved so deeply and then the opportunity for him to do so was ripped away leaving a horrendous gash in his heart.

I couldn't look at him while he was telling me the story of what happened without bawling my head off. It broke my heart to see this young man crying and asking over and over why it had to be her that died? Why did he have to lose her before they even had a chance to start their lives together? He was crushed and he was angry. He needed to get all this stifled emotion out and I was the person there willing and able to allow him to do so. We sat embracing each other as we cried together. Losing someone is never easy. I had suffered loss of a loved one many times throughout my life, so naturally I was empathetic to Brendan that night.

Once the flood of emotion had been released, it was like a ton of bricks had been lifted off of his heart. Of course everything wasn't immediately magically perfect for him, but the healing had begun! I feel very blessed and honored that I was Brendan's choice that evening. It is my belief that God will use a willing person in any situation to extend love, care, and compassion toward another. The people I met, like Brendan, weren't just some dollar sign to me. They were human beings with lives who been through some stuff. Brendan had been through recent hell and I was happy to help pull him out.

Rad Dude

Over the years I met some very super cool guys. I also met some pretty generous guys too. Rad Dude was superbly cool and incredibly generous. He came to one of my Seattle incalls for our first meeting. He and I had a few in depth conversations prior to our initial appointment. We learned quite a bit about each other. I learned about his really fun career choice and I told him about my life and my three kids.

He arrived to my little cozy suite and we had our first lovely little romp. It was easy to be with him because we already knew so much about each other. It felt like we had known each other for a long time because of the various conversations we had prior to our first "date"! After we finished our fun, he asked me if it was okay to give my kids a gift. I was a bit surprised, but said yes because I knew they would be happy to hear that they were receiving something from one of the guys I met, since usually it was me that received the gifts!

Rad Dude said he'd be right back in a few minutes because he had kept it in his car, not wanting to be presumptuous. When he came back, he had a shopping bag with the gift inside. It was what became the kids' first Xbox including a few games! I had mentioned that my boys didn't have one in a conversation that he and I had, so he decided to make sure they got one. Of course my kids thought that was pretty amazing for a person they had never even met to be thoughtful enough to bless them that way. They still tell people the story of where they got their first Xbox... The unknown faceless person who to them was so nice.

That wasn't the only thing my Rad Dude friend did for us. While I was trying to establish myself as Sandhal, I was having a difficult time saving money. I wasn't a "high volume" girl. I didn't like taking more than one appointment a day if I didn't have to, which meant I wasn't making a ton of money beyond basic living expenses. It was September and I was spending money for school supplies and clothes for my kids along with having to pay for all their extra-curricular activities they were involved with.

I still had temporary incall locations and was trying to find a permanent place. That is when I found the penthouse overlooking Lake Union. It was pricey, but I knew I could make it work because I was already forking out lots of money for the temporary places as it was. A permanent place would be cheaper in the long run. I was approved for the penthouse because my credit was decent and my accountant had kept stellar records of my financial affairs. The only problem I had was I needed first last and damage deposit for this place and I only had "first month's rent" saved up!

Rad Dude knew I had been looking for places and he called me one day to see how it was going. I shared with him how I had the perfect most amazing place for the kids and I and I'd be able to have my incall there without worry of detection. I explained that I didn't have the money to get in. He asked me how much I needed and I told him. He said he would contact his accountant and swing it for me. Within the next few days, he unconditionally gave me the money, and soon after, the kids and I had "moving day!"

Rad Dude was our hero another time as well with the same type of thing only this time it was after we had moved out of the penthouse to a smaller place. This was around the time when Sandhal had recently ridden off into the sunset. He paid our rent without any conditions set while I was trying to find work. The irony; I met him because he was "buying time" with me and there he was, months later buying time for my kids and I in a different way!

Chase

Sometimes I would receive a gentleman's request for him to spend the entire day with me. Chase, a California guy, was one of those men! He first contacted me asking if I was able to book with him for an eight hour date. Of course I had to do the usual check references thing with him. Since he wasn't a local guy who frequented the Seattle scene, I had to trust that the ladies names he gave me were going to be the type of girls who understood keeping each other safe and therefore be honest about this guy. After a few days or so I got really great replies from the women so we were good to go.

Before Chase and I met he told me he wanted us to enjoy a really nice dinner at a good restaurant, and asked me think about where we could go. I suggested a place that I had never been to but many people I knew had gone there. It's a restaurant on the water called Palisades in Magnolia, a nicer neighborhood of Seattle. I told him that they were known to have delicious food, great ambience, and I had heard that they had a koi fish pond in the restaurant.

All of the above were correct! Palisades was a hit! Our server was lovely, the entire staff was professional but fun and down to earth. You could see Puget Sound with boats floating by in the distance outside the windows. The dining room was dimly lit and nicely decorated. The fish ponds were tranquil and soothing while waiting to be seated.

The restaurant doesn't rush patrons through. We had a nice leisurely meal time which for me was something I hadn't had a chance to enjoy for many years. Since we took our time eating our way through the courses, there was plenty of time to chat. We talked about life stuff, his work, my kids, how and why I got into the business I was in, our favorite pop culture things, movies, and our favorite television show which for both of us at the time was "24"! He liked it for the intensity, storyline, and action. I admitted that though I really loved the show for those same reasons, along with it's innovativeness in how they allowed the viewer to see storylines unfold, I also had a longtime respect for Kiefer Sutherland, so watching him every week was enjoyable. We also ended up talking about foods we liked and didn't like and now have a goofy inside joke we share about shellfish!

Chase was tall with a stocky build. More of an "Average Joe" kind of guy, he was what I would consider most of my clients to be. However, hands down he was in the top five most charming of the men I met in those few years! He had one of the best senses of humor of all the men I met and we laughed a lot while we were together.

Chase and I were about the same age so we had a lot in common. He was single and hadn't had very good luck with dating over the years, so this kind of dating worked for him. It gave him the opportunity to spend time with a classy lady who he was confident could carry herself gracefully in public. That was me! He also knew that he could have some type of sexual encounter with the lady and though it might not be a permanent relationship, at least he felt cared about for a little while. I understood where he was coming from on that since my prior dating life never really led to something lasting. I feel like that was one of the main reasons I was able to be his temporary girlfriend experience and have such a wonderful time with him.

After dinner on that first meeting, we drove through the city a bit and then back to his hotel. He stayed in a very swanky older but classy place downtown. It was absolutely charming. The antiques in the common areas like the lobby and hallways were exquisite. His room had the most notable wallpaper I had ever seen! **Literally it was like classical sheet music tastefully pasted up throughout the room. It was lovely.**

I felt like I had stepped back in time; To the days where a woman such as I was referred to as a courtesan and respected as such, which in reality perfectly fit my persona as Sandhal

Banks! It was an elegant feeling! I had just sauntered through the hotel lobby and up the elevator with my gentleman friend. The front desk clerks, the bellhop, and the concierge all saw us walk by. They might have had their suspicions about me, but I didn't care! I knew I was headed upstairs with the man who, for the past several hours had been "courting" me and I was about to give him the royal treatment he deserved!

To my surprise, when we entered his room there on the bed was a gift bag waiting for me. Inside was a bottle of "Pure Poison by Dior"; my favorite fragrance! There was also a wonderful Disney collectible included as well. He had certainly done his homework and came prepared to make sure I was treated special! I returned the favor in my way for our remaining time together!

The next time we got together, we were supposed to go to a local car show and then to a nice fancy dinner, but when we got to the car show location, he realized he had the wrong dates and had come up from California for nothing... Well, also he came up for a visit with me, but the car show was the catalyst and main reason he visited Seattle that weekend! He wasn't too bummed at our sudden change of plans. We decided to go drive around and instead of some fancy dining, we went to the place that suited both of us far better; A casual popular burger place! I'm far more of a "comfort food" girl than I am a "fancy dinner where you have to be super proper" lady! I was able to be more myself comfortably wearing jeans and a cute tee shirt that day! It was definitely a day of really getting to be "just Marlee"! We had a genuinely fun time since we were now more like friends getting together. Of course, he generously gifted me more "Pure Poison" perfume and another super cool Disney collectible. In fact, it was something I had wanted for years that I had told him about when we first met and he managed to find it for me!

It was so enjoyable to hang out with him longer than the usual one to two hours that most of my appointments were booked for by other gents. It really was a great way to build a solid professional relationship and not have to be concerned with fighting or heartbreak. It worked very well for us.

We kept in contact via email and I saw him a handful of times before I retired from "Sandhalworld". We would always catch up and discuss the current or recent "24" season, and laugh with each other, making corny jokes! I briefly went back to escorting a few years back for a very few select clients, so I have seen him more recently than anyone else, but it still has been several years since I've seen him. Chase holds a special place in my heart because our friendship became real.

R. Grayson

While I was playing the part of "Kendra," I was sent out on a call very near to my home late one Friday night. Caryssa was annoyed with this particular client, because he had called late into the evening and was new to her service, so I had to ID the guy and make sure he was cool. I was fine with seeing him, but she could get testy sometimes, due to the nature of her business...

R. Grayson was a groovy guy! He was single, a smoker, and a definite bachelor with his taste in home décor. Our common ground thing we shared besides rock music, was our love for kitty cats. He even grew his own catnip and gave me little burlap bags of it for my cats!

When I went to meet him that night it was somewhat rushed because I knew I was going to be called out of the appointment by Caryssa earlier than the full hour of time he was paying for. She was not one to be generous with "time". I quickly got down to "business" to make sure that he would be happy and hopefully become a repeat customer for me! He ended up a happy camper lying there on his back. I can't remember exactly how it happened but while we were laying there talking, I ended up with a glass full of water pouring all over me; strictly by accident! It gave us a good laugh and led into a lighthearted conversation before our time together was over.

We started talking about creativity, productions and projects that either he or I had been involved in. I had been toying with an idea for a television show and I shared a few ideas with him to see what he thought. Somehow in our chatting that night, we both figured out we had a very good mutual friend! Small world for sure! We had a laugh about what we would say if we were ever around this person at the same time as to how we met. I told him that person already was aware of my current occupation and thought it was cool so I didn't figure they would judge him!

We exchanged phone numbers and decided that beyond that evening we would be better as friends rather than having a "professional relationship." He used to come over and help us with our computer or my website issues. He knew my kids, though I don't think the kids ever figured out that he was once and only once, a client of mine.

White Envelopes

Daine

One summer afternoon in my earliest days as Sandhal, I received a call from a guy named Daine, a new client, who was hoping to see me as soon as it could be arranged. Apparently, his friend had purchased time with another local escort for a birthday gift for him. His friend thought that since he was always too busy working, that he needed to get laid! When he phoned me he said that his recent appointment with the escort didn't go well; The girl seemed mechanical and not into it. Daine said he had done some research and found my reviews to be intriguing, and they were also consistent with regard to how I treated the men I met. The reason he wanted to meet me was because he wanted to be appreciated for his time spent as well as have a really good time. He seemed boyishly nervous over the phone but I agreed to meet with him a day or so later at my temporary incall near downtown.

Daine arrived on time in the late afternoon for our scheduled session. I heard the usual quiet knock at my door and went to open it, wondering what the poor soul who had been shown a horrible time by his first escort experience looked like... When I opened the door, ready to greet him with my usual warm and happy smile I did the biggest double take ever. For a moment, I thought it was Orlando Bloom standing there in the hallway! It was not, but he certainly did look very much like him. It was a very good day indeed!

With his movie star looks it was easy for me to want to dive right in. The girl he saw before was crazy in my book, but thanks to her I gained a repeat client who I will forever keep the memory of many amazing moments in time with!

The first day of meeting, our time together was off the charts awesome. Daine and I had no problem pleasing each other as we rolled around that room! We also had an engaging intelligent conversation with really great mutual connection. He was a business owner which of course would give him freedom in the future to take extra-long lunch breaks.

Unfortunately that first hour we spent together flew swiftly by. Daine had to leave to go to a barbecue for a friend's birthday, so he asked to use the shower. Of course I said yes. He took a quick shower and got dressed, combed his damp hair and said he was ready to leave. He kissed me, said thank you and started to open the door. As we were saying goodbye, he pulled me to him and kissed me more intensely, and then that was it... We were done... Off went the clothing and before we knew it we were wrapped around each other twisted up like pretzels!

Daine was late to the barbecue!

After that day, I saw him a few more times fairly close together. We had a physical connection much like one or two guys from my long past personal relationships. It was very difficult for me to keep my professional hat on for these afternoon trysts of Daine's and mine.

With everyone else I was always able to keep it professional even after the orgasms. The sex was always "just sex". Of course I tried to make sure it was personalized for each guy, but nevertheless it was clinical rather than personal, business rather than pleasure... Except with Daine.

I wasn't ever in love with him, but somehow when we were together it was so intensely awesome that it seemed more "real". The lines got real fuzzy from my perspective. It even got to the point where I told him that I couldn't accept the white envelope from him anymore because I was having way too much fun and it seemed far more like a "friends with benefits" relationship rather than a client to escort business transaction.

The next time I saw him, when we were finished with our private soiree and parted company, I was relieved to see that there wasn't an envelope in the place he usually left it. I went in to straighten up the vanity and shower and when I came back out, I found a white envelope had been placed behind an end table lamp. For some odd reason, it made me feel bad and I began to cry. That was when I realized I had crossed that invisible line that allowed my heart to open to feeling emotion like I would if I was dating someone rather than it being a simple exchange of money for a service...

The next time he called me to schedule, I told him I would only see him on the condition that he doesn't give me cash. He said he wanted to pay me in some way, so I suggested if he was going to visit that he simply bring a gift of some sort to me instead. So he brought me gift cards! For some reason that seemed to work well for me (and my daughter, who recently benefited from using a Nordstrom gift card I found in a bag not long ago).

Several months passed without seeing or hearing from Daine. I knew he had begun seeing a newer escort that had surfaced in our community. He even reviewed her often, something he never did for me which was fine because I had plenty of them out there anyway.

It seemed as though he was somewhat smitten by this girl.

One day I got a call from him asking to come visit. Of course I said yes. We had an amazing time like we always did. We never lacked physical chemistry for sure! Afterward when we were laying down and talking he told me he had a girlfriend. They had met recently and he said things were moving pretty fast and he was okay with it all happening in the way it was. I told him I was happy for him because he certainly deserved all the happiness life could bring.

Time passed and I hadn't really seen him or his presence in our community. The other girl he had been seeing disappeared off the forum too. I always wondered if she was the girl he fell in love with. I never got to ask him though.

He called me out of the blue probably nearly a year after the last time I had seen him to say he was getting married. I congratulated him and wished him very well in his new marriage. He asked me my thoughts about seeing married men. I told him that it isn't my business if a guy is married or not. Most clients I met I never really asked. If they told me they were married, that's how I knew. My profession was based on the things I was able to provide to men who had need for my service. That was my professional stance. So he asked me if I would still see him once he got married. I told him that any young man who becomes newlywed who feels the need to see an escort shouldn't be getting married in the first place. I said that sadly, I didn't feel I would be able to see him knowing he had a new young bride at home who would be trusting that he was monogamous.

That was the last time I spoke with Daine. He was the first guy to truly make me feel emotion strongly enough to break through the hardened professional barrier I had built around me. He was also the last guy in my life to make me feel that kind of emotion.

Here's the Story of Some Lovely Ladies

Seattle has a tightly knit community of providers. Every lady I had the honor of meeting was a spectacular human being. They were all very much like me in their care and compassion for others. Those women were such fun just to be around and hang out with. Many of them were single moms supplementing income to provide a good life for their families. Some were escorting to help advance their quest to have enough money to open their own shop, restaurant, gallery or other small business. A few did it so they could have the money to buy their own houses and be set for when they got older. Whatever they were wanting in life, these women were hardworking and driven to attain their goals. Some of the ladies just plain loved men and sex so it was a win-win situation for them! Some ladies had their businesses for a very short time and others for many years until, like me, it was time for them to ride off into the sunset. **Some of them are still working their alter-ego lifestyle even to this day!**

Most of the women I knew were really attractive and just absolutely delightful to spend time with! Some of these women were so dang funny and I had a blast just sitting and chatting with them! Though I never had a lot of time to hang out with these women, we all had a strong camaraderie and we would always have each other's backs because we all understood the nature of our profession.

The variety of ladies matched the variety of men out there; Just like the real world! Some of the gals were incredibly book smart, others were super creative. There were the hippie-zen types and there were the ladies next door. There were the super made-up runway model girls and there were the casual natural beauties who shined from the inside out! The youngest girl I knew of was just 18 and the oldest one I knew of was 52! Super tall to teeny-tiny short in stature, the ladies were thin or voluptuous, muscular, or had soft natural curves. There were several girls with fake boobs but I think there were more of us who just used what God blessed us with naturally! There was a plethora of beauties to choose from in that city for any man wishing to indulge in the companionship of a woman who was ready to make them feel like a king; even if only for an hour or two. If variety is the spice of life, then Seattle was the most flavorful escorting spice rack of all!

I didn't get to know very many of the ladies really well, but I was friends with a few of them. I even ended up doing "duos" with a few ladies. Those were always interesting for me since I didn't have a bi-sexual bone in my body. But I did have a hankering for money so I learned how to put my "game face" on and I guess you could say, "I kissed a girl and I liked it" (for the money I did, anyway)!

My Dynamic Duo
Partner & Friend

My closest friend within the community (besides Caryssa) was the one woman who I aspired to be like as an escort when I first started the business. "Austin" was beautiful and classy. Oh how the men adored her! She was never seen at any of the community mixers and kind of remained a mystery. She had an ability to attract the extremely wealthy clients on a regular basis; The kind who would whisk her off to some fabulous destinations around the world for both business and pleasure. She knew how to market herself bigtime!

It took me about a year as Sandhal to actually get to a point where Austin and I were able to chat on the phone and finally meet. One of us needed to contact the other for a client reference. I remember thinking, "I finally get to talk to the mysterious Austin!"

We had a really nice chat for quite a long time. We both expressed how much we each had high regard and respect for each other. We talked about how "one of these days we need to get together" and decided we were going to make it happen. As we were talking, she made mention that she happened to have tickets to an upcoming "Motley Crue" concert to which I shrieked and told her she was so lucky to be able to go. Then she said she didn't have anyone to go with yet and wondered if I would like to accompany her to the show. "Heck yeah," I said!

In the time before we went to the show, but after our phone conversation, Austin called me to ask if I would be willing to come to her house and have a duo session with her and one of her best clients. I told her I wasn't really into girls and she said she wasn't either but we didn't have to do much and we would make a lot more than our usual rates. That was enough for me to agree to the session!

A few days later, I went to her house, met her and her gentleman friend and we three had a little afternoon fun. It was a very interesting experience for me. She was right. We didn't really have to do much with each other for this gent to be happy. His desire to have two women give him full attention was more what he wanted rather than to watch two girls having sex.

I met Austin at her house the day of the Motley Crue show. We decided to leave early to be able to take our time getting out to the Amphitheatre, having time to grab a bite to eat and get some drinks along the way. Not too many drinks of course, but again, pacing ourselves so that when we got to the venue we wouldn't have to spend lots of money for overly-priced beers!

She had the top down on her convertible BMW and Austin definitely loved to crank her music and sing. There we were, Austin and Sandhal, two beautiful MILFs driving down the highway, singing and laughing and having a blast! Near the venue, we found a good parking spot on a side road where we hoped we'd be able to get out easily after the show and we headed into the venue.

Once we got in there we found our seats, but then went to go see about getting drinks. We found some guys willing to buy our drinks for us (Imagine that!) and we chatted with them for a bit, thanked them and parted company since they weren't seated near us.

The opening bands played and they were cool, but we were there strictly for Vince, Tommy, Nikki, and Mick! The band had guys with video cameras moving around through the audience to capture their fans doing weird, funny or outrageous things. Of course they were finding all sorts of young girls willing to lift their shirts to reveal their ta-tas to the world... Sissy stuff for Austin and myself. We started making out and groping each other and putting on our own show for the people around us! I have no idea if we ever made the "Crue cut," but Austin and I had a crazy little moment there that we'll always be able to reminisce and laugh about!

After that day, Austin and I had opportunity for more duos. Her guy had put the word out in the hobby community about his outstanding time with the two of us. We booked more appointments after that and shared some great moments together. She and I mastered the art of fun with each other without really having to do the things we really didn't want to do.

Over the years we've kept our friendship going. She is the only girl from the community that I keep in touch with now. We both have gone through some heavy stuff over the years and we both share the experience of working in the taboo industry of escorting.

Though we don't connect as often as I wish we would, every time we do so, we pick up like old friends do; as if we haven't missed a beat. We get caught up on our kids' lives and each other's lives. We're both out of the business now. She stayed in it longer and came out of it set up far better off than I did. That didn't surprise me at all!

Why Men Visit Girls Like Me

For years we've seen the bad rap men take when there is a high profile bust involving any kind of prostitution. They get ridiculed and scoffed at. Their lives for a while are usually turned upside down and inside out. The lady or ladies involved usually end up with 15 minutes of fame and then fade back into the unknown...

The men who seek out women who give their time and companionship in return for money are usually lacking something in their lives. In all the stories about the gentlemen I interacted with that I've shared throughout this book, they all had desire for something that they weren't able to attain at home.

Many of my clients were just plain lonely. A good majority of the single guys were at a point in their lives where they didn't have time for cultivating a relationship, but they would reach that point of just needing to feel a woman's arms wrapped around them and receive an intimate connection with someone. Sometimes sex became the bonus they received along with feeling wanted or needed, even if it was only for that small window of time. For others it was the warm hug, a tender kiss, or a sweet gaze into their eyes from a caring soul that gave them the reassurance of their value to get them through until their next time of need.

I had several guys who never even wanted the sex. They just wanted me to hang out with them. They just needed me to be there; to be their friend and confidant. They had nobody in their lives that they could share their deepest thoughts or their most personal desires with so they'd spill it out to me. I listened and it went no further...

I was a friend to the lonely when they had nobody else.

Some of the guys like Brendan who I shared about before were at a super low point in their life. They were sad or broken-hearted due to a situation that was not in their control. They had suffered great loss of a love, a family member, their job, or maybe even a lawsuit. They lacked the love they so badly wanted or needed. Solace couldn't be found at home. Inner peace was buried by turmoil...

I was able to give comfort to a wounded weary soul.

Lots of men have fantasies they wish to play out. They might want to role play or play dress up and act out a certain scenario. Some want to play out a more normal life situation, others enter into a kinkier realm wanting to try the most sexually taboo kind of play. Some are single and have nobody to play with. Some have wives or girlfriends who would never attempt to try anything out of the norm and possibly get offended or be appalled at the suggestion.

I was able to fulfill their desires safely and discreetly with no judgement.

So many men shared their unfortunate stories of being ignored intimately by their wife. I know women get tired, and they don't get the help they might want or need with chores, and the kids drive them crazy, and the dog barks too much, and their co-workers piss them off or annoy them, and the noisy neighbors give them headaches which makes them never want sex, and, and, and, and... BUT, I say, C'mon ladies! Enough with the excuses. If you don't want girls like me to stay in business then don't give your husbands any reason to seek me or my other lady friends out. Men need that sexual release. It's true that they think about sex hundreds of times a day. They will go in search of it if they lose it at home, or at the very least, be tempted to find an outlet where they can be sexually gratified.

I was the sexual partner when they had to go and find one.

Most of the married men I met with loved their wives immensely. They never talked of wanting to leave their wife. They enjoyed being married. They just felt they were "never enough" for their wives. They didn't do their "honey do" list right, they didn't make enough money, they didn't help with the kids enough, they didn't say the right things, the car never worked right, the house was too small and on and on... The husband would get tired of being wrong or doing things wrong and they would just give up and withdraw. The wife would shut down emotionally and the marriage line of communication would snap. I heard many stories of situations like this during my time as Sandhal.

I accepted them unconditionally just how they were and they were always enough.

Bring Your Sexy Back

Men seek out a woman like me because they know we provide a service that will include giving them whatever it is that they are lacking in their personal private life.

They know with an escort there will be no emotional head games. They're confident that they are going to get the sexual release they need and want without having to deal with attitude from a woman who is annoyed that she has to "put out" some type of obligatory sexual activity for them. They're excited that the woman they have paid hundreds of dollars to isn't going to fake an orgasm because she wants to have a real one as badly as he does and will show him how to make her do so if he doesn't know how to already on his own!

I've never understood how a wife could have her husband and his willingness to be there in bed with her every night and not want to enjoy him in a sensual, loving fashion or get a bit more playful and do cool and freaky things together. Having a guy want to share the same bed with me night after night for longer than a few months would cause me to happily jump in bed with that guy and rock his world every single night and several times in between those times until I die!

All marriages deserve to have what I refer to as, "Wild Monkey Sex"; the kind that is out of this world mind-blowing! The "no words" indescribable, intense intimacy with wild abandon-type sex! Or even silly, fun, playful sex, or whatever kind of sex a husband and wife feel like creating as often as possible. Keep the fire burning!

There are so many women out there who are married but have no sex life with their husband except when she wants something for some gratuitous reason. I have several friends who fall into this scenario. What really annoys me is that I know of women who give their husband the gratuitous sex, the annual birthday or special occasion sex, or the "I want something" sex and then their husband leaves them cash or a credit card on the counter the next day as a thank you... Really? That is the exact same thing that an escort receives from a client so technically, many wives are actually no different than a prostitute when it comes to their sex life... They just have a ring and piece of paper that makes it legal! **Harsh but true reality.**

If that hits a nerve, don't get mad at me... Do something to change it. Get that romantic wave flowing again. If you don't feel good about yourself, then figure out what it is that will bring some personal happiness back. Start working out. Proven fact; Exercise will release endorphins that make you happy (Have you not seen "Legally Blonde"!?) Take a personal enrichment class of some kind, stand outside in the grass for 10 minutes a day to ground yourself with earth, walk on the beach, go sit at a park, try a new recipe, enroll in a class with your spouse. Get out of your comfort zone. Let yourself feel good!

Once you start feeling better about you, your confidence level boosts and your happiness meter rises. You begin to feel better, look better and yes, your "sexy" starts to come back. There are many resources available out there. Find things that work for you, but you must simply try. Don't forget that laughing at yourself is a great thing! That has been my lifelong mainstay.

Life After Sandhal

My personal accountant Harry had set me up as a small business during my years of escorting. I paid my taxes every year as a business owner. I was set up first as an escort, then as an event planner, since at times I did that on the side. I also did some costuming for musicals and other creative projects. Luckily I had all of that to place on my resume so there weren't any gaps in job history. Obviously, I omitted my years working as "Sandhal" on my resume so I didn't have to explain my "job description" as an escort to potential new employers!

When I began my job hunt after ending my escorting business, I quickly realized how difficult the search for new employment was going to be. I was going from a job that paid me $300-$400 an hour, to regular jobs I was "qualified" for that started at around $9 or $10 an hour at the time. I couldn't even make in one eight hour day what I was able to make for an hour of my time spent with men! In fact, it would take a 40 hour work week in a "normal" job to make as much as I could in one hour having sex with a stranger! For the next six and a half months I was unable to get hired at any of the many interviews I went on.

As the months passed, I ended up getting further behind in my bills. My brother managed to help me get rent paid through a couple of sources like his boss' community charity, and a local coach friend of ours. My brother and a friend of his were going to be opening up a restaurant. He said his friend had asked me to help with their menu. I spent over 100 hours on that menu creating several new recipes and designing the menu with a creatively worded sports theme. His friend paid our rent that month I was told, in return for my time of constructing the menu. Unfortunately the restaurant never did open, but at least my kids and I didn't get evicted...

The next few months my kids and I were saved by my friend Bridget and my former client turned friend, Rad Dude! One paid our rent for the month of August and the other for September. Unfortunately I still had no job by the time October rolled around. What bit of savings I had dwindled down to nothing. I was completely broke. The manager of the apartments we lived in on Queen Anne was as kind as she could be, but to keep from jeopardizing her job, she had to ask us to leave or an eviction notice would be next.

Sheer panic set in... Of course, I contemplated, I could always "resurrect" Sandhal and she would be able to pull in lots of money...

Instead of me going back into escorting, my kids and I ended up homeless and sleeping in our car! Being homeless in October in Seattle wasn't ideal. It was cold, wet, and rainy outside. We had all four of us and our cats inside the car. Not the most ideal situation, but we had each other and we were safe. That's what mattered most. Sleeping in our car ended after a couple of days. We bounced from one temporary living situation to another through the kindness of friends over the course of the next six months. Eventually I bit the bullet and humbled myself enough to ask my dad if we could live with him. My dad welcomed us and within a few days the kids and I finally ended up at my father's house which was my childhood home.

At the time, Brittnee was a senior just graduating from high school. In late July of 2007 she moved to Southern California to pursue a career in acting while working at the most known theme park in Orange County. The boys and I stayed up in Seattle. I found a good place to work as an administrative assistant through my brother's friend Betty until January of 2009 when we had opportunity to move down to Orange County and join Brittnee who was living near Anaheim.

California:

Where Dreams Can Come True

Things didn't work out quite the way I had hoped when we relocated to The OC. The door to the job I had been hoping to get for years was slammed tightly shut. It was devastating, but I knew there had to be some reason or purpose why things happened the odd and unexpected way they did. I floundered for the next few years after that trying to find the path I was supposed to take.

As nothing seemed to work for me except finding a few jobs where I made just above minimum wage, I became determined to finally begin my quest to share my story. Finally, I was really going to write and self-publish my book once and for all! I had told so many people over the years that I was writing a book and I had started it.

At about 120 pages into my writing, my pc crashed and I lost nearly three quarters of the content as I had not backed it up anywhere! Frustrated, I shelved the book idea for a few years until all of a sudden one day the words just started flowing. It became so easy to write and the reality of a finished manuscript was in my reach. For the first time in eight years everything began falling perfectly into place!

That is when you know you're on the right path!

How I Kept it Real

My encounters weren't raunchy meaningless affairs. I was known as a GFE which is an acronym for "Girlfriend Experience." Being friendly and engaging is naturally how I live everyday life. From my very first appointment, how I portrayed myself was always simply as "just Marlee," even though I had to use a made up fantasy name.

Most of the time, especially when I was on my own as "Sandhal," more often than not, I would end up telling the client my real name. I chose at my discretion who would get to know me as Marlee. If a client learned my real name, it was because he treated me kindly and with respect. I wasn't treated only like a body they'd paid to have sex with.

My friends would ask me why I would tell my clients my real name. Obviously for protection and discretionary purposes having a public fake persona was wise. I reached a point though with my repeat clients where I figured since I knew their real names, addresses, and most of their workplaces, that they could know mine as well. Kind of an ironic gesture of building trustworthy professional relationships in an industry filled with deception! It worked for the type of person I strive to be in my personal life.

For me it was just too weird when I was kissing a guy or in the heat of passion the guy would say, "Yeah, Sandhal," or "Do you like that Sandhal?" or whatever he would express. It was worse when I was "Kendra." That name did not suit me in any way! I was happy when I got to choose my name. I picked the name Sandhal after my favorite Broadway dancer of the same name, though spelled differently!

I am actually a fairly decent actress, but in the heat of the moment as a guy was exclaiming,

"OH SANDHAL!", sometimes I would snap back to reality and have to fight back huge giggles because it would just strike me funny; I was laying there with a stranger totally naked and "doing it" and he didn't even know my real name. The way my mind worked within that scenario is that some song like the "Cheers" theme would pop up in my brain at the point in the song where they sing, "Where everybody knows your name and you know they're glad you came." And that's where the giggles would start to emerge! Then before I burst forth with laughter, consequently ruining the poor man's ego, I'd whisper to the guy, "Hey, my real name is Marlee. You can call me by my name."

*I was real, genuine, and candid. I couldn't be anyone but "me."

You Really Can't Judge a Book By It's Cover

What I learned through seeing countless numbers of men over the course of nearly four years of escorting, is that there truly is beauty to be found in everyone. Unfortunately, I had those rare occasions where I had to look really hard to find the good in a guy. If all else failed like I mentioned before there was always that white envelope placed on my table that gave me something positive to focus on!

There were men I spent time with and had sex with who in the real world I probably would have never have said yes to had they asked me out for a date. Many of those men ended up being some of my best encounters because they were kind, funny, generous, smart, and some of the most genuine down-to-earth people I was ever lucky enough to meet. I learned that it matters not what shape or size someone is or how they look in outward appearance. It is the very soul; the eternal energy inside each person that truly counts. Obviously there has to be some type of physical attraction, but with different perspective, one can meet and instantly view a person as intriguing, beyond the physical outer shell.

As long as they were super squeaky clean and smelled good they could look like the Hunchback of Notre Dame or Phantom of the Opera and I didn't care! I definitely learned that you can't always judge a book by it's cover... Sometimes you must pull that outer cover off and pilfer through the pages to see what interesting tidbits are inside!

There were guys from time to time who booked appointments with me strictly for the sex and didn't want small talk. There were a few who got my "GFE" style of service confused with "PSE" (Porn Star Experience), thinking that I was a screamer and an acrobat and liked it rough. I would try and set them straight or sway the activity, but if it didn't go well, then I wouldn't allow them the pleasure of seeing me again.

There was a guy I saw only once who was one of those really rich younger guys in one of those cool uptown high rises. He was tall and handsome and I thought he would be lots of fun. He really only wanted PSE sex, lots of sex, and he wanted me to do some very odd things including having me tell him in a baby-talk voice a bunch of very naughty adult things!

My first thoughts when he presented that special request was, "What baby would ever even know how to say the things he wanted me to say?" Then he told me he would throw some extra money my way, so naturally I obliged him. Talking like a baby for a few minutes was worth an extra three hundred dollars. The years of sexual abuse and conditioning I had endured helped me in these odd moments in my escort career... AND... It's amazing what a few glasses of wine will help you to do. Well that and a few extra "Benjamins" for being a good sport and playing along. Wealthy, handsome guys can be some of the biggest weirdos! That's not a bad thing. It's just something I concluded as I look back analytically on my clientele.

Being an escort helped me gain great confidence over time. Knowing that men were willing to pay $300 to $400 an hour to spend their time, many for multiple hours, with me was a pretty huge ego boost. To be able to command a certain rate and have people want me that much to pay me for my service was flattering and amazing!

An escort, much like a hairdresser, becomes a counselor or life coach during the appointment time. Because we experience intimacy with people, that often leads to hearing life stories; sad tales about marriages gone flat or bad, stories of misfortune, family, and so many other topics of discussion. A compassionate caring escort will assess a gentleman and allow him the time to express and get things off his chest. On many occasions I was able to do that.

To entice clients to book appointments with me, I often used my creativity. Once I made spinning wheel of fortune so when a gent came over, he could spin the wheel for a chance to win a free booking or monetary price reductions off of his session and other little bonuses. I held a few food drives during holiday times where if a client brought a certain amount of food items to be donated to the local food bank they would get to pick an envelope that had some type of discounted prize inside. Not all of my gentlemen friends were rolling in dough, so money saved for them was a good thing and it was another way to make them happy! It was a bit of whimsical fun to share with my clients.

Escorts are thoughtful and have kind hearts!

More Than Just Sex

After watching me trying to finally begin dating again and instead meeting a bunch of jerks from the online dating scene, Brittnee saw firsthand my confusion with men. If I met a guy I really liked I would try to just date them without getting anywhere close to having sex with them. If I didn't have sex with them after the first few dates, I never heard back from them again. The guys I ended up meeting and sleeping with would be done with me after one or two romps in the hay. It seemed I couldn't win in this middle-aged dating game any better than I could when I was in my late teens and my twenties.

When the contemplation of whether I should become an escort or not began, Brittnee said to me, "This is a no brainer, Mom! All guys seem to want you for is sex, so it seems only fair for you to make them pay you for it!" She was only 13 years old at the time, but saw how I could take all the rejections of the guys I had tried to date and turn my new way of dating into something profitable for me. Capitalizing on the sex without the chance of heartbreak.

During that same conversation, Brittnee and I delved deeper into the concept of why it was that I couldn't seem to find a man to develop a relationship with. I was fun-loving, kind, generous, witty, and had lots of love waiting to be shared. I was in really good shape, and kept myself looking sharp and trendy. My kids were engaging and fun to be around. They weren't trouble-makers. They were involved in school activities and were helpful in our community. We were a good little family.

Apparently without realizing it I was giving out sexual vibes since that's what I seemed to attract; sexual behavior. As we were beginning to research the world of escorting and we were talking about how sex is all guys seemed to want me for, we came to the conclusion that I was actually more than just sex and it was time to let everyone know it! That day we developed a concept for a variety type show called, "More Than Just Sex With Marlee."

We actually began gathering friends who we felt would be great for our production team. We held a few meetings to brainstorm various segments we could include as well as what the set might look like. We started writing scripts and storyboarding. We even talked about the new concept of a "web show." Unfortunately, before it even got off the ground, one by one I lost my team until it was back to just Brittnee and myself. That's when I went full speed ahead with my escorting!

Many times since then she and I have visualized and talked about the show coming to fruition and we know that someday the avenue will be there. Until then, I'm happy to share and teach information through my speaking engagements.

Honesty Builds Team Strength

Something I did for my kids that lots of parents don't do, was be completely honest with them within the boundaries of their ability to understand and comprehend something. If life was peachy, they knew it. If we were broke, they knew about it. I was never one to try to keep up with the Joneses or Smiths or anybody else for that matter. Allowing my kids to see that I had financial struggles, I was able to meet those tough times head on, showing the kids my willingness to work hard to make sure we stayed afloat. Even though we ended up without a place to live for a short time, we learned to be strong and forage through. To this day, my kids are hard workers who take their responsibilities seriously and they don't give up easily either.

My boys didn't know at first that I was an escort, but it only took them a few months to figure out that my job wasn't normal. On their own they each asked me about my job. Why I went to people's houses and how come I came home with lots of cash every night. I explained that I was an escort. I told them that I basically got paid to go on dates with men and they paid a lot of money for me to look pretty and pretend to be their girlfriend. They both seemed satisfied with that answer for the next few years!

Of course Brittnee knew what was going on. She and I worked very hard on learning as much as we could about what I was getting myself into. She was much more savvy on computer than I was so her ability to hunt and search for websites was quite helpful. Being able to code basic HTML gave her the knowledge necessary to build my first website for me via the old dinosaur we knew as Netscape!

I always figured if I was honest with my kids that they could trust me enough to be honest with me as they grew older. We've always been ridiculously close, my kids and I. More often than not, we were all each other had to count on so we've always had each other's backs.

I kept my kids safe. Even though my incall was in our home, my clients and kids didn't not interface. On occasion, they would pass by a person who they thought might be a client as he was leaving our building. They would just walk nonchalantly by the guy. They used to giggle if they had seen someone they thought might be the one who I had just seen. I always told them it could have been, but most likely whoever they had passed was just another tenant in our fancy lake view building!

If the kids were around when I had an upcoming session, they would go downstairs to either the Starbucks or Taco Del Mar that were on the ground floor where we lived. I would give them money for food or drinks so they could have something while down there. They would wait until I called them to inform them that the coast was clear and they could come back up! For them it was a bit of an adventure. Almost like they were secret spies. They had fun with it.

Brittnee was in high school at the time. Several of her friends knew my occupation. I was definitely one of the cool moms in the PTSA according to them. I was very involved in my children's school careers and activities. I had to be cautious of who knew what I did for a living. I never wanted my kids to be outcasts because of my choice of work. For the most part I was just another, regular, average mom.

There was one time when Brittnee's close friend Shauna called her and said that her mom received an anonymous email that had been sent to her, the school principal and various others stating that "Brittnee's mom is an escort" with a link to my website. Her mom thought it was atrocious that someone would say such horrible things about me and try to hurt me like that. She didn't know what I did for a living, and we don't think she ever caught on that I really was an escort, but nevertheless, I had been "outed"! At first we panicked. Then after talking about who might have done it, we all concluded it could only be one person. Most likely due to high-schooler jealousy of Brittnee and Shauna's close friendship. Luckily no fallout ever landed. It just went away and my business carried on!

Brittnee and I often talked about how my work was simply a job that I enjoyed. Having my own business was something I had to work hard to sustain, but at least I was happy with my life and knew how to cope. Unlike so many of the other moms we knew, I was able to live life without popping prescription pills or consume any other kind of drugs. The moms in our community would sit and chat amongst themselves about which pills they were on and why. They would whine and complain about their woes; How they weren't going to be able to have their house remodeled that year or take their exotic vacation or how their husbands wouldn't do this or that right and it was so stressful for them, blah, blah, blah… I would lean over to Brittnee and joke, "And *this* is why their husbands come see me," and we'd have a little laugh!

At the time, my boys for the most part were too busy in their young teenage lives to even realize what I was really doing. They knew the basics and that was best for them at their ages. All three of my kids were involved in school musicals and plays so that kept them busy beyond their school days and the homework that came with it. My boys also played football, basketball, and baseball so their plates were always full. They stayed out of trouble because I had taught them manners and how to behave respectfully toward others. I also made sure they learned to have self-respect for themselves that I lacked as a child!

Toward the end of my short career as Sandhal my oldest son and middle child Michael, in a concerned voice, asked if he could speak with me about something. I said of course and asked what was up. He told me that is was bothering him that I was meeting with men because he finally realized what I was having to do to make money and he didn't want me to have to do that anymore. He was just a couple of weeks from turning 15. He had begun figuring out what I was doing in my appointments with men, due to what he was starting to feel toward girls his age. I asked him if he wanted me to quit and he said he did, so I told him I would. This was a good mommy decision, with poor timing!

I knew I had to at least try and stay in Sandhal mode for a while to save money, but my heart was tugging in a different way. That conversation with my son was the intro to my mental and physical preparation to walk away from my life as Sandhal. Within a few weeks I was done. When I told Brittnee who was just about to turn 17 and my youngest son Steffen who was six weeks from his 14th birthday, they both agreed that though we'll be struggling to get by it was a good thing for me to say goodbye to my life as Sandhal.

Many years have passed since my career as Sandhal was going strong and successfully in Seattle. The honesty and openness along with always taking my kids thoughts and feelings into consideration have allowed us to remain very close to each other.

We all live in Southern California now and are living life to the fullest! The kids are all grown up and have turned out to be well loved young adults who are respected by everyone that surrounds us. They are currently pursuing their own individual goals and following after their dreams to be successful in their chosen fields.

All of them are pursuing careers in the entertainment industry. My daughter is a working actress in films and television, my oldest son is working in family entertainment, and my youngest son has his sights set in recording his music and music production for others. They all work hard at regular jobs while trying to reach for the stars and I am very proud of all three of them! It's all in how you approach a situation that will dictate the outcome! I was always honest with them and I was hard working. They have turned out to be the same.

How Could You?

To those who ask me, "How could you do such a terrible thing since many of the men are married?" I say this; Men came to me lacking or needing something in their life. It mattered not to me if they were married or single. I wasn't the homewrecker. The home is already wrecked if the married guy is coming to see me!

The person you need to concern yourself with is the one out there hoping to steal your boyfriend or husband because they are crushing on him, are having an actual affair with him, or have fallen in love with him. The escort doesn't want your husband. The escort has a business as a service provider and she really only wants to make money from him; She wants the white envelope!

I view myself no differently than my friends who are massage therapists, florists, or hairdressers. People go to a professional in a particular field because they know what they are doing. I provided a service just like a hairdresser or florist would. You need a nice hairstyle? Go to stylist who has a good reputation for cutting hair very well. You want to send flowers to a sick friend? Seek out the florist with spectacular flowers! You need good sex? Find someone with a good reputation who can perform that fantastic service for you too! You wouldn't want me to cut your hair because I'm not well trained in that. I am however very well trained on how to have amazing sex! With the lifestyle I had from my earliest memories until now, sex is and always has been what I'm best at. Well that and cooking or baking so maybe someday I'll write a cookbook or have a cooking show!

In Time Healing and Victory Do Come

I have no guilt or shame at all for anything that's happened to me or for whatever things I've done... That's because I have an understanding of God's forgiveness toward me. He doesn't get offended by our screw ups... People get offended, but God doesn't.

God is Love... Love doesn't get offended!

There will be people who may lash out over my honest and genuinely candid expression of my experiences I transparently share and they may not like or agree with my choices. I do not apologize for being "me." It's who I am. I never claim to be perfect. I'm far from that. I'm just sharing a very important part of my personal world with the entire world in hopes of people gleaning whatever they can from it whether that be insight, fresh or new perspective, healing, forgiveness, freedom, the ability to laugh at oneself, or whatever lightbulb moment that might happen while reading along.

Though in some ways it wasn't the wisest lifestyle, and I know it wasn't a perfect career choice for most people, the fact remains, God never left my side at any point. He didn't hide in the closet peeking through the louvered doors or cover His eyes with embarrassment because I was naked with strangers doing all sorts of crazy-assed things. He was present with each encounter that I had and during every sex act I performed! It was He who gave me protection beyond what condoms ever could. Never once did I contract an STD as an escort and after more than 10 years post escorting, thankfully I am HIV negative. I trusted Him as I entered into that world and he had my back the entire way.

When I had my conversation with God about what I was embarking on as I was preparing to enter into the world of escorting, I just simply told him that I know that he already knew that I would go down this path. I was confident that he would protect me and my kids. I guess I had an intuition that someday there would be victory for me somehow in all of this.

Victory came to me in the most wonderful way through my decision to become an escort and take control of my sexuality. I had finally learned that my body was mine and nobody else's. Whatever a guy feels or felt sexually toward me is NOT my fault. His hard-on was not my fault. It's a physical thing that happens when a guy gets turned on, but my being sexy or attractive or just being myself living life doesn't make it my fault and it certainly does not make me "obligated" to do something about it for him. We all must be in control over our own bodies. Self-control is a good "fruit" for each individual person to bear.

Nobody ever had the right to guilt me into thinking I had to fulfill their sexual desires. Those who paid for me to spend time with them met me when I was at a point where I was trying to gain back the control in my life that was taken from me at such an innocent age. The only obligation I felt with clients was to make sure they left smiling because the service I provided for them was excellent. I was a sex provider because I chose to be one. I had spent 35 years of my life giving my body away to guys and not getting a whole lot back for it (except for three phenomenal children)! The ability to turn it all around for my financial gain gave me control. Finally, after all those years of being used or abused, I had what I now refer to as "pussy power!"

On different occasions throughout my life prior to escorting, I must mention that I did meet people who I ended up liking and dating who were really nice. Unfortunately for me they were too nice. I was so used to being treated poorly by the majority of the guys I encountered that when someone actually was sincere in their feelings toward me, I shunned them; turned them away, or just allowed the relationship to fizzle out.

I couldn't handle the genuine guys. It was an uncomfortable feeling knowing that they were sincere with no expectations. I had no clue how to accept someone's love without them asking for anything in return. It was a tremendously foreign concept in my life that truly freaked me out (My theory on why so many girls like "bad boys" is this: Examine the childhood of a girl like that and I'll bet you find a "wounded bird." In some way she will have gone through a traumatic experience like abuse or suffered a severe loss).

I never really stood a chance of being "normal" whatever that is!

I remember so many clients asking me why I wasn't married. How could I not be married when I was so fun and engaging and loved to laugh and was a good mom and enjoyed cooking and baking and having lots of sex and so on. They would chatter about me being such an amazing potential wife. My answer was always the same, "I don't know." I still have people who ask me now why I'm not married... My answer has changed to this; "I don't know. I don't get out much!"

Back then I was wanting to date and it didn't ever go well. At this point in my life I'm not really wanting to play the dating game. I'm not looking for "Mr. Right" either. If someday it happens then it will be great. I have become super picky on what I want and if the guy is out there, I know God will allow us to bump into each other somewhere. He'll hopefully either be some former 80's hair band rock star, or someone sexy to me like John Cusack, Kiefer Sutherland, or Keanu Reeves. A girl can dream... And I am a dreamer!

After my Sandhal escapade ended, our life was a struggle including having those few homeless stints. I gained weight and felt awful about myself because so much of my life had been based on how I looked. For years I felt unattractive and became unhappy because of that. I stopped allowing pictures of me to be taken because I felt I was super ugly. The harder I tried to get back in shape it seemed the more weight I gained. I remember several times of struggling financially and thinking if only I could resurrect Sandhal... But with my extra weight, there was no way I was going to allow any guy to see me naked! I was no longer that girl who was comfortable in her skin able to prance around all happy and carefree.

Lately I have been able to analyze and come up with a theory about the weight gain. Though I don't believe God does mean things to us, I do believe He will allow for certain things to happen, in my case gaining weight, so we can learn or grow stronger in our character. My weight gain prevented me from going back to my Sandhalworld that was so tempting. Escorting was only for a season in my life, not to be a permanent lifestyle. It taught me much and allowed me to heal and grow and learn many things about life, humanity and myself. Once that chapter closed, the temptation to open it back up was huge, so the middle aged weight gain fell upon me and stopped me from going back into escorting.

Now, several years later, the weight has begun to come off fairly easily and I feel pretty snappy in how I'm looking again! I'm over 55 years old now, so I certainly don't expect physical perfection; That would take too many surgeries and fake synthetic materials being pumped into my body to look "better". It just doesn't seem worth it to me when my food choices and working out will do what's best for my health. Age happens and I want mine to happen naturally and gracefully. Sexy is a state of mind and I still have it!

Currently there is no temptation to bring Sandhal back, though I have always joked about doing so because $300 - $400 an hour is far better than my ridiculous $10 - $12 an hour jobs I've had since then! It was very difficult to go back to the "real world" of working very hard for minimum wage or just barely over that at a job where you earn a paycheck in order to pay rent and bills to barely survive. The adage of finding something you love to do and figure out a way to get paid for it is the key to my true happiness. The little jobs in between are great for stepping stones to stay above water. I'm still incredibly happy and grateful for the wonderful blessings in my life. My "Life's Lemons" are always turned into amazing lemon meringue pies or luscious lemon bars because that's what I choose to do with those lemons!

Opportunities to coach other people's relationship difficulties in regard to sex have occurred for me over the years. I've always said that though I'm not very good in the love connection, I am very good in the sexual connection. I'm also great at teaching people how to communicate in the bedroom and under the covers. Technique, energy level, and desire to be totally into it are very important elements for successful sexual encounters. If a person doesn't know how to acquire those things on the spot for spontaneity sake, I love to help them figure out why and how they can get there! My wish is for all couples to have amazing relationships with sexual tenacity that gets more amazing for them each year they are married rather than losing their sexual appeal for each other over time for whatever the reasons might be... Communication is the "key."

Love Doesn't Label, Love Simply Loves

I've been called a lot of names in my lifetime... I used to take it personally and allow labels to dictate who I was and how I viewed myself. I've been called a slut so many times that I just call myself a slut like others might call themselves a dork or doofus or something like that! The origin of the word "slut" came from the Middle English word "slutte" which meant a woman with an unkempt kitchen or a naughty kitchen maid... The irony is that I really do not like it when my kitchen is a mess but I am naughty like a kitchen maid!

I had a person once ask me how I could call myself a Christian and be an escort at the same time? They said I was a slut for doing such horrible things. They asked how could I on one hand be such a slut and still say I love Jesus? How could I be a Christian and sin like that?

I thought it over for a few moments before I spoke and proceeded to answer their question with a question; I asked them how they could still call themselves a Christian and still lie, cheat, be gluttonous, act jealous, get angry, be a gossip, judge others or do whatever it is that they do in their weakness that falls in the "sin" category? Sin is a sin is a sin... Christians are all still sinners. Humans are sinners! I believe God works all the garbage out of us in His perfect timing as long as our hearts remain open to the voice of His wisdom. To those who still feel like judging my transparencies I simply echo this; "Let him who is without sin, cast the first stone..."

Soon after that conversation happened, one afternoon Brittnee and I were joking about that whole judgmental ordeal. We discussed people's perspectives and how so many people think that as a Christian you are supposed to be perfect and do nothing wrong in life which absolutely sets people up for a huge fall because perfect humans do not exist!

I've never felt the need to justify my actions in choosing escorting as my occupation. That was a great personal decision for me as it was the road which eventually led to my awareness of truth in who I am and what I'm really here for. I had found a way to make money at what I was good at and for a temporary time it was exactly what I needed to advance my life beyond the mindset of unworthiness I had lived under for so many years before. For someone who didn't have a college education, I was able to have my own business that sustained a high quality lifestyle for my three children and myself. I was proud of how well I built up a solid business with a fabulous clientele.

I enjoyed getting up every day, seeing my kids off to school or driving them there myself. Then I'd workout, hop online to check my emails, work a bit on marketing myself, and then meet with my client of the day. When they walked out the front door, I would have the rest of the day to do whatever else I needed or wanted to do whether it was chores, head out to watch my boys baseball or football games, cook dinner, go shopping with my daughter, bake some cookies, or watch TV. For me it was a very normal enjoyable lifestyle.

Being called a slut when I was younger certainly hurt my feelings. To say it's fine that people called me such a harsh name would be me displaying kindness to those who might need a little extra grace in their life! Over the years I learned to embrace that label and rock it like nobody's business! I've since decided to *own* the word "slut"! It's my word; the word that actually prompted me to share my secret world with everyone to help take power away from the very people who know nothing about me and people who have walked similar paths as mine.

While there are those people in my past who have called me names with intent to hurt me or make me feel bad, I don't really fault them for thinking that way. Even if people view me as such during or after reading this, that is completely their freedom of choice! I am who I am and I approach all that comes my way with the mindset of "It is what it is," and I move forward as gracefully as possible. I am not defined by anyone except God and He views me as His perfection.

I have weathered things in my life that many others would have crumbled from. I've been thrown into the depths of life's trenches and have belly crawled through the muck right out of them. Through the storms, I have zig-zagged my way up to the top of the mountain that I stand proudly on top of today!

My belief is that Jesus' love isn't exclusive to the perfect do-gooders, the holy and more righteous-than-thou folks, or those who try desperately to follow every single rule to get closer to God. He will be right by your side wherever you are at and in whatever you are doing. He is omnipresent!

God is easy! Religion complicates him. Humans make him hard.

God gives His love freely because He himself is Love. Love forgives. Love doesn't keep a record of wrongs. Love does not judge. Love is everything that is "good." Jesus is Love. Jesus easily loves everyone right where they're at; Love is... LOVE.

The knowledge of Jesus' love at a young age is what gave me the strength to endure the dark points throughout my life. Understanding the spiritual power of the Creator, God, Universal Being, or whatever you choose to view as your higher power if you have one can be the difference of getting through a tough situation and coming out of it positively.

Growing up the way I did and constantly searching for true love led me down so many interesting and exciting paths. Experiencing the world of escorting I suppose is to be considered the most outrageous journey in my life so far. Without knowing what the future holds I'm not sure if I can ever top that one! However, I'm confident that God will be with me on whatever adventures I choose to go on. Although I have yet to find true love in human form, I have discovered God to be my "consistent perfect love". I am completely content with that.

I'm operating with a concept of using wise choices to guide me, but I also know that the crazy "fly-by-the-seat-of-my-pants" adventures are always around the corner. The question is, do I turn left, right, or continue forward to the path leading me to the next mountain to climb so I can discover another new life view!

For me I guess the direction doesn't matter. What matters most to me is that I intend on enjoying the adventure, I will learn something along the way. No matter what happens, I know God has my back, my kids love me, and I love them; We are still a team and cheer each other on in our attempts at achieving goals and dreams.

I am still the same as I always have been, though maybe a bit stronger and wiser. I'm still a person who wants to be loved, wants to love others unconditionally as best as I can try to. I desire to be kind and helpful in ways I can to those who I cross paths with. I still love sex (Or the idea of it anyway... It's been years...)! Also, I still love to laugh and do so all the time. It is and always will be my strength to get me through whatever life brings my way.!

See your beauty and you'll always be beautiful.
Know your value and you'll always be valuable.
Show your love and you'll always have love.

~~*~~*~~*~~*~~*~~

Acknowledgements

I wish I could individually list everyone here who has impacted my life in a positive way. In life there are no chance meetings, so everyone who I've ever interfaced with has helped to get me to this very moment. The people with the positive input are who I thank the most!

I am grateful for all of my family and friends who have loved me through the best of my life as well as the toughest parts; to all who travelled through the trenches along with me; I love you.

My kids; Brittnee, Michael, and Steffen; We four have stuck together through it all and have made such a strong and courageous, yet amusing, talented, and loving "team" over the years. Thank you for being such wonderful contributors to my life and this world. I'm so proud of all three of you and look forward to all that life has in store in the years to come. I love you the most. Team Gee forever!

My dad Lee; Thank you for your unconditional love and for being there to help when need be for whatever the reason. I know it wasn't easy once mom went on to Heaven, but you did your best. I love you Dad!

My brother Lorin; My original p.i.c. What lives we've had! They could name a roller coaster ride after us with the zany adventures we've experienced! Thanks for helping out through the years. Love ya little brother! (Go Hawks!)

My sister Bonnie and her husband Scott; Thanks for all the support and help in the early nineties. It allowed me to be there for the kids in those crucial formative years. Thanks for everything. Much love.

My relatives on all sides; I hope this book brings clarity to all of you and you better understand who I am and why. Thanks for your love and understanding. Love you all.

My closest lifelong friends who have loved me (and prayed) over the years no matter what choices I've made; Michelle, Cara, Lisa L; Thank you! You three have given me such joy over the years!! Laughter, tears, FUN; We hold dearly such great memories of fond times. So many of my darkest moments became brighter just by thinking of our friendships and all the great years of memories we share!

Pam V; Thank you for being my "secret sister" and using your God-gifts! And for everything else!

J & C, Barb P, Kimberly KBS, Lisa K, Chris and Nancy, Karen R, Karen D, Pam K; Memories of fun times, conversations, and friendships strengthen me along the journey!

Lisa, Jaz, Alexa, and Ana, you four were our family when we had no one close. You housed us twice at such crazy times in our lives! We will always be grateful! Pancake wishes and Chocolate Cake dreams to you all! (Dinosaur!)

My daughter's BFF's; Hannah Oh! & Katie P; Thank you for your encouragement for this project. More importantly for being such fabulous friends and more like family for all of these years!

Mike B; Without your computer, we would still be formatting!

My stellar group of contributors:
My Super Heroes - Brian E, Rod & Yolanda R, Brittany H, Stine E, Grant S, and Roxie R.
My Amazing Heroes - Ashlee B, Brian and Dana R, and Justen T.
My Big Heroes - Seattle Siren, Don Decanter, Seattle Yujin, Karen D, Katie P, Simone A, Shannon B, Manon V, and Tomi J.

Thank you for helping this dream become reality! Your generosity and patience will always be treasured and remembered!

Made in the USA
Lexington, KY
30 March 2019